Information Service
Excellence
Through TQM

Also available from ASQC Quality Press

Creating a Customer-Centered Culture: Leadership in Quality, Innovation, and Speed
Robin L. Lawton

A Quality Transformation Success Story from StorageTek
A. Donald Stratton

Breakthrough Quality Improvements for Leaders Who Want Results
Robert F. Wickman and Robert S. Doyle

Principles and Practices of TQM
Thomas J. Cartin

Excellence Is a Habit: How to Avoid Quality Burnout
Thomas J. Barry

The ASQC Total Quality Management Series

TQM: Leadership for the Quality Transformation
Richard S. Johnson

TQM: Management Process for Quality Operations
Richard S. Johnson

TQM: The Mechanics of Quality Processes
Richard S. Johnson and Lawrence E. Kazense

TQM: Quality Training Practices
Richard S. Johnson

To receive a complimentary catalog of publications, call 800-248-1946.

Information Service Excellence Through TQM

Building Partnerships for Business Process Reengineering and Continuous Improvement

Timothy Braithwaite

ASQC Quality Press
Milwaukee, Wisconsin

Information Service Excellence Through TQM: Building Partnerships for Business Process Reengineering and Continuous Improvement
Timothy Braithwaite

Library of Congress Cataloging-in-Publication Data
Braithwaite, Timothy
   Information service excellence through TQM: building partnerships
for business process reengineering and continuous improvement /
Timothy Braithwaite.
      p.   cm.
   Includes bibliographical references and index.
   ISBN 0-87389-271-2 (acid-free paper)
      1. Information resources management.   2. Management information
systems.   3. Total quality management.   I. Title.
   T58.64.B73   1994
   004'.068'5—dc20   93-47481
                                                                  CIP

10 9 8 7 6 5 4 3 2 1

ISBN 0-87389-271-2

Acquisitions Editor: Susan Westergard
Project Editor: Kelley Cardinal
Production Editor: Annette Wall
Marketing Administrator: Mark Olson
Set in Avant Garde and Janson Text by Linda J. Shepherd
Cover design by Montgomery Media, Inc.
Printed and bound by BookCrafters, Inc.

ASQC Mission: To facilitate continuous improvement and increase customer satisfaction by identifying, communicating, and promoting the use of quality principles, concepts, and technologies; and thereby be recognized throughout the world as the leading authority on, and champion for, quality.

For a free copy of the ASQC Quality Press Publications Catalog, including ASQC membership information, call 800-248-1946.

Printed in the United States of America

 Printed on acid-free recycled paper

ASQC
Quality Press
611 East Wisconsin Avenue
Milwaukee, Wisconsin 53202

To all those who
would make a difference

Contents

Foreword

If you are interested in some practical advice on how to apply TQM principles to improve the performance of an IS department, this is the book for you. Tim Braithwaite has put his years of hands-on experience as an ADP auditor, a system development methodologist, and a security officer together with his experiences as manager of systems departments to produce a readable and to-the-point primer on how to apply TQM thinking in an IS setting. He gets to the essence of the IS improvement problem quickly, and makes specific recommendations whose beauty lies in their consistency, unity of purpose, and directness.

This is a serious book. IS performance is too often derided in the press and denounced in the boardroom for it not to be taken and treated seriously. The trend to client/server computing that is downsizing many IS departments by moving application development out to the end-user organization is not eliminating the problems, just moving them around. Production quality application systems of consequence do not happen by themselves. They are built by organizations that follow sensible and effective procedures and that pay attention to the needs of their customers and their employees. The recommendations offered are not simple to implement, as they involve the core competencies and behaviors of the organization. But they are the right recommendations, in that they get at what have been proven time and time again as the reasons IS departments fail to perform or to meet management expectations.

This is a positive book. It offers a great deal to the reader who adopts its philosophy and acts to apply it in his or her local environment. I think you will enjoy reading it. I know you will find lessons in it worth applying to your organization.

Philip J. Kiviat
Director of Federal Marketing
KnowledgeWare, Inc.
McLean, Virginia
September 1993

Preface

This book presents an application of total quality management (TQM) philosophies and principles to the business of defining, constructing, and delivering automated information systems and services. The objective is to prepare the centralized or decentralized information services (IS) department to participate fully in the quality improvement and enhancement initiatives of the enterprise. In meeting this objective the responsibilities of the IS department are viewed as threefold.

First, the IS department must set and achieve high internal standards for the continual quality improvement of their systems and services. Without a reputation for providing quality service, the opportunity to influence the direction of future customer improvement and enhancement initiatives is greatly diminished.

Second, the IS department must support its customer's (user's) goal of delivering quality services and products to the ultimate revenue providing customers of the enterprise.

Third, as the rest of the enterprise gets more deeply involved with TQM, business process improvement and enhancement activities are likely to experience great difficulty unless the IS department is an active and willing partner in the effort. After all, how many business processes are not already dependent on automation to some degree? It is with today's automation that many quality problems and inefficiencies lie. It is also within the realm of automation that many future quality improvements and efficiencies may lie. In such cases business process improvement initiatives must take existing automation into account, which cannot occur without the full support of the IS department maintaining the current systems.

In a closely related sense, and using today's *in* terms, those who would *reinvent, reengineer,* or practice work process *obliteration* on government and business would be well advised not to minimize the dependencies that currently exist on automated systems and on those who service them. Further, these popular concepts, in practice, will most likely focus on the automated elements of a *new way* of doing business; but they will rarely provide sufficient attention to the impact that the *new way* is likely to have on the employee in the workplace, the organization, or the customer.

A systematic application of TQM principles during reengineering efforts will provide just such insights and will help ensure that the totality of the workprocess and workplace (that is, things other than the computer) is analyzed for impact and changed, if necessary, to be in harmony with the automated elements.

This book was written primarily for those involved in the IS support function. These groups are referred to organizationally in many different ways to include management information systems (MIS), information resource management (IRM), information technology/systems/services department or division, local area network management, or data center. For ease of illustration, I have chosen the IS department as the frame of reference since it includes, in most organizations, all of the functions of providing information systems support to a customer.

This book also addresses and places into perspective the important obligations of the customer (user) to the success of an information systems support project. For the user the responsibility to define requirements has always existed and has always been difficult. Historically, users never really understood the need for the detail that they were continually being asked to provide during a systems design. Now, with the advent of TQM, and its focus on work process analysis and evaluation, users are better equipped than ever to participate in the analysis and design of the automated portion of their work process. The need for detail is better understood and users are now capable of providing such detail within the overall context of their workprocess and business activity.

This book can also be used by the business manager and quality specialist as a guide for ensuring that TQM *thinking* is being applied during the development of future projects involving automation. Used in this way, the TQM principles of customer focus, design of error-free workprocesses, preventive thinking, and employee involvement will result in a clearer and more precise statement of requirements; while the principles of cost of quality and adherence to standards and measures assist in the efficient delivery of systems and services that meet those requirements.

Finally, the implementation of a TQM initiative in the IS department is seen as creating some very favorable opportunities for promoting the value-added contribution that the IS department can make to the enterprise. The manager who embraces the principles and philosophies of TQM, who uses the language of quality to build bridges to the customer, and who improves the systems and services of his or her department will win the confidence of top management and be able to make a sustained contribution to the future success of the enterprise.

If you need further information about TQM in information services, you may contact ASQC at 800-248-1946 to request the author's address or telephone number.

Acknowledgments

For the development and production of this book, I feel a deep sense of gratitude to the following people:

- My many teachers, students, friends, and colleagues, who understand the importance of their professions and strive daily to "do it right"

- My wife Kathy and my children Kelley and Jonathan, for their love and support and their ability to ensure I keep a real-world perspective

- My parents, whose sense of compassion for all people has served as a dependable beacon in this age of technology

- My sister, a true believer in the goodness of all people

- Ron, and his sense of what can really be accomplished

- Ned, who will never let me quit before the finish line

- My friends and colleagues in the business, who believe there is a "pony in the room"

- The professionals at ASQC Quality Press, whose patience and encouragement is greatly appreciated

- Diane, who would never do less than a quality job

Introduction

"Quality is the key to making American products. We are in the midst of a technological revolution, and our work to build quality products will be a crucial link to the long-term success of the United States in the global marketplace." This statement by former President George Bush set a direction for the nation and correctly identifies the important role technology will play in reaching this goal of building quality products.

The technology, projected to be at the center of these long-term quality improvements, is information services technology in all its many forms. In an information-dependent world the vast majority of hoped-for quality performance and productivity improvements can only be as good as the quality of the information and service available to direct and manage the business activities of the enterprise as a whole.

This book addresses the relationship between quality of information and the quality of business products, and services. More precisely, it addresses the quality of information produced from automated information systems and presents the case that until the philosophy and principles of TQM are consciously and systematically applied to the development and management of automated information systems, the quality and productivity and performance gains hoped for by many enterprises will be marginal at best.

Recently, under President Bill Clinton, this same executive-level commitment to quality and technology has been demonstrated by numerous initiatives, including the National Performance Review led by Vice President Al Gore. To quote President Clinton, "The desire and necessity to improve government systems and the identification of TQM as a means of improvement are only two parts of a three-part problem. The third part is committed and determined leadership to make those improvements comprehensive and continuous."

TQM provides a solution to the quality, performance, and productivity problems of any business activity, but each activity has a unique set of environmental conditions that define it, and perceptions and expectations against which it is measured.

Chapter 1 will explore the conditions, perceptions, and expectations under which the IS department operates as it attempts to fulfill its charter. This chapter will set forth the premise that many IS groups have, over time, lost sight of the true criteria by which their success is measured. Chapter 1 will attempt to define the IS department problem for which TQM offers a solution.

Chapter 2 will introduce the reader to the philosophy and principles of TQM, as viewed from the perspective of an information technologist attempting to apply TQM to the business of information systems development and management. The discussion of TQM principles will be presented as a summary of the consultations and materials developed by the LEADS Corporation of Greensboro, North Carolina. The consolidation of the various theories into practical TQM guidance belongs to LEADS. Interpretations of that practical guidance belong to the author as I have attempted to apply them to the information services community. I do not support one theory over another, but I am convinced that even a small application of any of them could begin to improve the quality of information systems and services to the great benefit of the enterprise as a whole.

Chapters 3 through 6 will attempt to answer the question, *What does TQM provide the IS manager?* The answer, I believe, is to be found in the following analogy.

> There is only one way of seeing one's own spectacles
> clearly and that is to take them off. It is impossible to

focus both on them and through them at the same time.
(*source unknown*)

TQM provides the IS manager with a way to systematically examine the internal processes of the IS department in order to improve the outputs of the organization. Improving these outputs contributes to the enterprise's efforts to improve its goods and services. These chapters will propose a practical implementation of TQM guidance using contemporary system methods, tools, and techniques, within the management environment of the IS department.

Chapter 7 will suggest organizational activities that can aid in TQM implementation as well as skills and attitudes needed to create a quality-oriented information management culture.

Chapter 8 will project a future of opportunity where the considerable value of the ISD can be realized. Because of the TQM connection, this will be a future where chief information officers survive more than 24 months and are finally seen by peer executives as making substantial contributions to the bottom line of the enterprise. A bit ambitious, perhaps! Perhaps not!

1 Perceptions of the Information Services Department

View from the User

It has been said that perceptions are everything. This seems especially true when it comes to information technology. On the one hand, our society heralds information technology as the solution to many enterprise inefficiencies that will reduce costs and increase profits. On the other hand, much is written that judges information system departments with poor performance and return on investment. As recessionary pressures have mounted, managers have been forced to reassess every dollar they spend, especially those spent on information services (IS).

> Let me tell you what I've come to expect from systems development projects: "They take twice as long as promised, cost twice as much as anticipated, and provide half the functionality they were designed for in the first place." That is how one jaded end-user described his experience with the project life cycle.[1]

Many in the IS community would snicker that our *jaded end-user* had a reasonably good experience. As Figure 1.1 illustrates, end-users are dissatisfied and oftentimes greatly inconvenienced by the introduction of technology into their organizations. Dissatisfied, because the

1

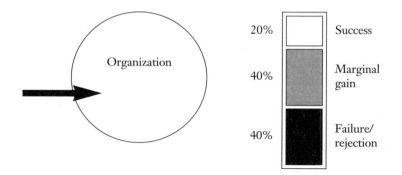

Source: Adapted from Ken Eason, *Information Technology and Organizational Change* (London: Taylor & Francis, 1988), 12, 33, 55.

Figure 1.1. Success rates in information technology application.

technology system often does not assist in improving the efficiency of job performance and seldom lives up to what was promised. Inconvenienced, because, all too often, users must devise *work arounds* to keep the work flowing despite the technical system.

The dominance of this reality is continually evidenced by headlines and editorial columns in information technology journals, albeit sandwiched between advertisements and marketing articles declaring how the next technological *widget* will be the answer to all your problems. For example, a few titles follow.

"Software Glitches May Delay FTS Recompetition"

"C-17 Program Plagued by Software Problems"

"IRS Programming Goof Stymies Crime Fight Effort for Two Years"

"Computer Problem Cited in Crash of F-22 Prototype"

In the private sector, software and system failures are not as highly publicized as those in the public sector. But, that is beginning to change as courts increasingly hold firms liable for losses caused by computer system errors. For example, consider three real-life technology nightmares.

In February 1991, hackers penetrate the computer network of Atlanta-based Equifax, Inc., a major credit reporting bureau that sells 450 million reports annually. Consumers' files, credit card numbers and other confidential information were accessed.

A computer system at SHELL Pipeline Corporation fails to detect human operator errors. As a result, 93,000 barrels of crude oil are shipped to the wrong trader. Cost of the error: $2 million court award.

A software bug causes a THERAC 25 therapeutic radiation machine to deliver a lethal dose of x-rays, killing a 33-year old Texas oil field worker.[2]

"Today, with computers controlling almost everything," says Susan Nycum, an attorney specializing in computer law, "there's a tendency for courts not to excuse the computer, but to hold responsible those in control of it."[3] So, we can see that while society's view of the power of technology is practically unbounded, at an individual information systems level we are not overly impressed with the results to date.

Peter Drucker, in his recent book, *Managing for the Future*, has several things to say about this state of affairs from the perspective of productivity improvement.[4]

The investment in data processing equipment now rivals that in materials processing technology, that is, in conventional machinery with the great bulk of it in services. Yet office and clerical forces have grown at a much faster rate . . . and there has been virtually no increase in the productivity of service work . . . the first question in increasing productivity in knowledge and service work has to be: What is the task? What do we try to accomplish? Why do it at all? The easiest, but perhaps also the greatest increases in productivity in such work come from redefining the task, and especially from eliminating what needs not be done.

This issue of what needs to be done and what needs not be done is at the heart of many automated information system problems.

It may well be the case that much of the confusion and frustration experienced in the implementation of information systems stems from the fact that the division of labor between the person and the computer is poorly thought out and mismatches commonly occur.

Figure 1.2 illustrates the initial and most critical element of analysis to which any prospective project must be subjected. *Just because a computer can conceptually do something does not mean that it should.* The exception is with real-time process control applications where the human element has been purposely *designed out* of the application and

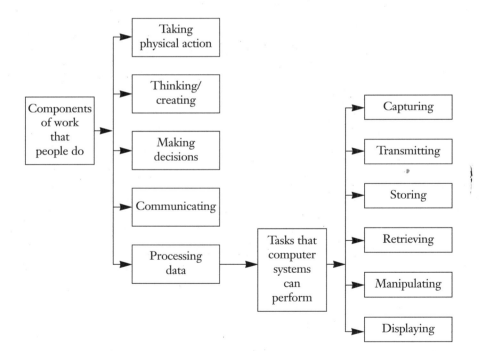

Source: Steven Alter, *Information Systems: A Management Perspective,* © 1992 Addison-Wesley Publishing Company. Reprinted by permission.

Figure 1.2. What computer systems can do.

consigned to the computer. In the vast majority of applications the components of work that people do should not be automated; only the supporting data processing tasks are appropriate for automation and then only after careful definition. This definition, following a full analysis of the *people-work* component, demands a much greater degree of detail than if the functions were to be done by a person. The binary nature of the computer requires a binary solution where the many nuances of human execution of the task must be spelled out in extreme detail. True, these data processing functions, when automated, will be accomplished faster and handle greater volumes, but the expense of instructing a computer to do them is also far greater and time consuming.

Because of the extreme specificity required to program a computer and the overall complexity, uncertainty, and confusion in the automation marketplace (that is, lack of standards adherence, insufficient testing, poor to nonexistent documentation, and so on), many individuals find themselves spending an inordinate amount of time and effort in the *care and feeding* of the computer! This often occurs at the expense of doing the people-work component of the job. Or worse, it is done in addition to the people-work component, thus leading to disgruntlement, burnout, and a very real dissatisfaction with the information system that was supposed to make their job performance easier.

Figure 1.3 illustrates the elements of design that must be considered in building an information system for human consumption. While reasonably equipped to *wrestle* with the technological elements of the system, you will find that most system developers have little or no cognizance of the key elements to the center and right of the figure. Is it any wonder that most systems are not considered successful by their users. According to Drucker,[5]

> In making and moving things people do one task at a time. But . . . where most knowledge and service people work there is growing splintering. The people at the very top can sometimes concentrate themselves . . . but the people who actually do most of the knowledge and service work—engineers, teachers, sales people, nurses, middle managers—carry a steadily growing load of

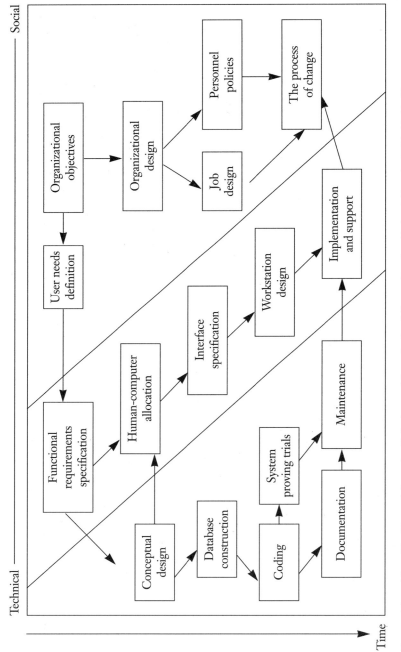

Source: Adapted from Ken Eason, *Information Technology and Organizational Change* (London: Taylor & Francis, 1988), 12, 33, 55.

Figure 1.3. Design topics in the sociotechnical systems design of systems.

busy work, additional activities that contribute little or no value and that have little or nothing to do with what these people are qualified and paid for.

No small amount of this busy work can be attributed to the care and feeding phenomenon and to the need to work around systems in order to get the job done.

> This is not job enrichment, it is job impoverishment. It destroys productivity. It saps motivation and morale. Nurses, every attitude survey shows bitterly resent not being allowed to do what they went into nursing for and are trained to do to give patients care at the patient bed. They also, understandably, feel that they are grossly underpaid for what they are capable of doing while the hospital administrator, equally understandably, feels that they are grossly overpaid for the unskilled clerical work they are actually doing. The cure is fairly easy, as a rule. A few hospitals have taken the paperwork out of the nurses' job and given it to a floor clerk . . . all of a sudden, these hospitals had a surplus of nurses. The level of patient care . . . went up sharply. Yet the hospital could cut the number of nurses needed, and could thus raise nurses' salaries without incurring a higher nursing payroll.[6]

This would appear to be a classic case of assessing the impact of information technology on job performance and realigning the execution of the automated functions to increase effectiveness and user satisfaction. It is possible to design an information system in this way when sufficient attention is given to all aspects of Figures 1.2 and 1.3. This is actually an example of business process redesign where mismatches are eliminated for greater efficiency.

View from the Bottom Line

The issue of efficiency and effectiveness of automated information systems is beginning to be subjected to the same scrutiny as the rest of the activities of the enterprise.

Donald Frey, former CEO of Bell & Howell, recently addressed this issue in an article by Jon Van of the *Chicago Tribune*. Frey, who has first-hand experience with this reality since he sits on several corporate boards, is quoted:[7]

> There seems to be a rather small impact of computers on efficiency. People are starting to ask, "How does this relate to the bottom line?" People who are lay people— non-techies—are saying, "Wait a minute, here's a $5 million bill for something. What happened to the $20 million we've spent over the last several years?"

While this discussion deals with a question of efficiency, more likely than not a similar discussion could deal with the plague of cost overruns that typify IS projects. These overruns are the staple of General Accounting Office (GAO) reports concerning governmental information system development efforts. Several hundred such reports have been published in the past decade. Figure 1.4 illustrates the most common cause of cost overruns found in these reports. There are many factors that lead to cost overruns. These factors include poor estimating methods, lack of trained

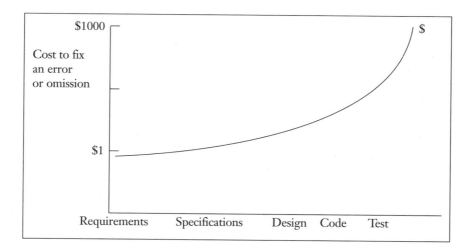

Figure 1.4. Relative cost to fix an error or omission.

and experienced staff, failure to manage the integration of the technologies of the system, lack of experienced project management, failure to validate requirements in early phases of development, and so on. Figure 1.4 in fact is the result of these other failures, and it is these other failure areas that total quality management (TQM) is uniquely designed to address. The GAO in a recent survey of an audit of 132 systems identified $7 billion in cost overruns. That's billion with a *b*!

The first analysis of this reality comes from a study by Barry Boehm in 1976. That study was based on data from TRW, IBM, and Hewlett-Packard. In the 1982–1985 time frame the data in Table 1.1 were collected and reinforced the earlier findings of Boehm.

The guidelines in Table 1.2 are observed potential and actual dollar amounts experienced by several companies and averaged.

By any measure these numbers indicate severe problems in the development and management of information systems resulting in an adverse effect on the bottom line. These numbers also point out deficiencies in the procedures used to develop information systems, a lack of management of the development effort, or a combination of both.

The Linchpin Phenomenon

These numbers, however, are only the tip of the iceberg. These numbers only reflect the cost to finally make the automated system right. It

Company	Specif. design	Programming	Testing	Install. & Maint.
IBM/Raleigh	$10	$100	$1000	$25,000
IBM/Rochester				$8000 ($10,000)
Large LA firm		$900	$19,000	$19,000
Hewlett-Packard	1 unit	10 units	100 units	Infinity
IBM/Santa Teresa	1 unit	27 units	64 units	127 units

Source: Adapted from Vern Crandall, Ph.D., *The Cost of Effectiveness of Software Testing Making a Case to Management* (Mountain View, Calif.: Sun MicroSystems, Inc., 1992), 45.

Table 1.1. Cost of finding errors at various points in the software development life cycle.

does not begin to account for the costs borne by the user in trying to perform mainline business activities with systems that are wrong and cannot be trusted. This ripple effect is especially acute where information systems are integral to daily business activities. With many business functions, the quality of goods and services is directly linked to the quality of information and automated support services.

A lack of quality information and poor automated service can contribute to inadequate enterprise decisions, poor quality products, and poor customer service. This dependency between the quality of IS department goods and services and the enterprise's goods and services creates what can be referred to as the *linchpin phenomenon.*

For example, at the customer contact level an inaccurate address for a package delivery service, resulting in a late delivery, contributes to a poor quality image for the company. At the middle management level inaccurate or incomplete information about staff skills and knowledge may lead to poor recruiting decisions that ultimately jeopardize a project's timely completion. Again, the quality reputation of the company suffers. Finally, at the executive planning level poor data collection and analysis concerning the assessment of a new technology and the stability of potential suppliers result in late implementation of a new product or enhancement. The corporation loses a planned competitive advantage and wastes limited resources.

Faced with the reality of increased competition and customer emphasis on cost and quality, corporate leaders have begun to ask a variation of the question, *What are we getting for our automation dollar?* The new question is, *How can automation be used to improve the quality*

	Specif. design	Programming	Testing	Install. & Maint.
Guidelines	$10–$100	$100–$300	$500–$1500	$10,000–millions

Source: Adapted from Vern Crandall, Ph.D., *The Cost of Effectiveness of Software Testing Making a Case to Management* (Mountain View, Calif.: Sun MicroSystems, Inc., 1992), 46.

Table 1.2. Guidelines for the cost of fixing errors across the software development life cycle.

of corporate products and services and give a competitive edge? In a later chapter, and based upon TQM philosophies and principles, we will explore how automation can solve not only problems, but can be used to pursue challenges and opportunities.

View from Within the IS Department

Before leaving this discussion of perceptions, expectations, and conditions, let us explore the feelings of the people within the IS department. Let us pose a few general questions and see if we can project some possible answers.

- How is morale in most IS departments?

- Do people aspire to excellence or to just getting by?

- How do the readily evident problems with quality affect esprit de corps?

- Do IS department personnel feel valued by the rest of the enterprise or as a group to be tolerated?

- Do IS department personnel, in fact, value their own work?

- Do IS department personnel feel competent to perform their job?

- What is the level of loyalty among IS department employees?

These are very difficult questions to assess directly. Answers generally have to be inferred based on user attitudes, and how organizations deal with personnel, turnover rates, and training statistics. To say that an ambivalent attitude exists toward IS department personnel may seem to be extreme, but not by much!

To support this position, consider the salaries paid for a service as dismally perceived as those in Figure 1.1. Nowhere else would a 20 percent success rate, or an 80 percent marginal failure rate if you prefer, be tolerated while payroll checks continued to be generated for the perpetrators of the service. By this measure one out of five fast-food hamburgers would end up in the garbage and two in 10 new homes would be unlivable upon occupancy.

With this image of apparent incompetence uppermost in the collective mind of enterprise management, what kind of signals are being sent to members of the IS department? There appear to be at least three subtle, or not so subtle, signals at this time.

First, the outsourcing movement has made a great many IS department personnel nervous. Never mind that outsourcing is often an admission, out of frustration, that *in this company we cannot produce quality information services efficiently, and we have given up trying.* The reaction at the IS department level is one of chagrin and anger. *Time to update the résumé.* Management uttering *outsourcing* pronouncements would be well advised that such talk quickly results in a self-fulfilling prophecy of poor quality and low productivity. You only thought you had a quality problem until everyone started looking for a new job.

Second, dateline *ComputerWorld*, 1992, headline "Kiss U.S. Coders Goodbye—foreign competition will put American programmers out of work unless our development, quality and productivity go up and costs come down." Now the threat is survival itself. Programmers are not to be merely moved around within the domestic economy; the work is to be shipped overseas just like many other American industries.

Additionally, a largely ignored reaction to the lack of quality information services is the increase in liability cases in the courts. While such suits would generally be against companies providing service for a fee, it may now be possible for such companies to sue their IS employees as professionals. "By signing on as members of professional IS associations, thousands of programmers, analysts and others have unwittingly made themselves liable for mistakes they make on the job . . . moreover, computer law experts say, those same workers could now be slapped with malpractice suits, just as lawyers or physicians who agree to abide by professional standards . . ." explains Daniel Brooks, a Washington, D.C., attorney and computer law specialist. "Because these codes hold members to certain professional standards of conduct, it makes a signed membership card a nail in the coffin when it comes to proving liability."[8]

The real answer to quality and productivity problems lies not in blaming, threatening, or suing the IS employee. It lies in changing the environment within which IS employees must function.

> Yourdan "blames U.S. programmers for rotten systems, crap code and not having a decent data processing

education. Bull. Blame the people who control the situation: management. Management sets the tone and determines strategic goals. Management is responsible for a company's (or division's or project's) success of failure. Management sets deadlines, dress codes, corporate educational policies and even determines if incompetents stay in the company."[9]

W. Edwards Deming certainly supports this notion. He contends that 85 percent of all quality problems occur as a result of policy, systems, methods, and procedural failures implemented and tolerated by management.

Ask university graduates with degrees in computer science the first thing they are told on their first job. The answer, very often and sadly, is that *you can forget all you learned in school, we do not do it that way here.*

Recently, *ComputerWorld* conducted its sixth annual job satisfaction survey. This survey, published in the September 14, 1992, edition made the following main points.[10]

- Heavier workloads and higher stress levels are reported by nearly two-thirds of respondents.

- Satisfaction tends to drop the lower in the organization you go.

- Three out of every four say they would welcome a job change.

At a personal level, . . . a surprising 85 percent of respondents say that happiness in one's job matters more than career advancement. Things such as sense of accomplishment, enjoyment of work, sense of worth and yes, money, are more important, they say, than simply getting ahead. [This would support a *techie is human proposition* and would force one to ask how well IS organizations align with this rank and file view?]

[Again from the *ComputerWorld* survey:]

- *Department satisfaction is down.*

   . . . 30 percent of all the respondents said they believed satisfaction in their departments as a whole was eroding. Nearly 35 percent of non-managers noted a decline twice the rate cited by management.

- *Few believe that IS is being used to its fullest potential.*

   Some 68 percent of all respondents say they believe that they are not working up to their fullest potential. The feeling is even stronger among non-managers (72 percent).

- *IS performance is seen as declining.*

   Some 15 percent of those polled described IS performance as declining versus 12 percent the previous year. Again, criticism was harsher at the lower levels with 21 percent of non-managers reporting a drop.

- *Many are looking for new jobs.*

   Although the hiring market is pretty dismal . . . more than 75 percent of those polled say they would welcome a job change. 20 percent are actively looking for new work. Among non-managers, those who said they would switch jobs rises to nearly 83 percent. Overall, the responses suggest that satisfaction is lower and criticism stronger at middle management and professional levels. This is probably because of staff cutbacks and workload pressure.

How stressed are you? More people say they feel more squeezed. Why? Increased workload—74.6 percent, increased demands from business—41.3 percent, concern about job loss—38.6 percent, budgeting constraints—37.6 percent, overall economy/recession—20.1 percent. What to do? According to respondents, flexible job scheduling, more bonuses, better training, more opportunities for advancement, better salaries, the opportunity to telecommute, and more feedback from supervisors could all help improve satisfaction."

Summary and Conclusions

Certainly the need for quality, productivity, and morale improvement exists in the IS department. Potential solutions to specific problems are plentiful, but the question of organizational readiness poses the real challenge. To determine the correctness of a course of action, we must analyze the environment in which the action must take place. Quoting our earlier analogy,

> There is only one way of seeing one's own spectacles clearly and that is to take them off. It is impossible to focus both on them and through them at the same time.

Chapter 2 will summarize a proven, pragmatic, and successful approach to TQM taken from the consulting practice of the LEADS Corporation. In chapter 3, we will use the philosophy and principles presented in chapter 2 as the foundation for the creation of a TQM program for the IS department.

2 A Generic Treatment of TQM

Introduction

The purpose of chapter 2 is to present a working concept of TQM that can be used throughout the remainder of the book. These concepts originate from the work of the LEADS Corporation, a TQM consulting company. The definitions have been distilled from many years of experience and meet the collective intent of the various writers on TQM.

Definitions and Terms

TQM is defined as a management process to instill a culture of continuous improvement in an organization. Such improvements will balance productivity increases against established quality criteria.

The principles of TQM can be categorized as follows:

- Recognize the need to improve goods and services.
- Meet requirements by focusing on the customer.
- Set error-free work as the goal for all activities.
- Manage by prevention.
- Identify and monitor the cost of quality.

- Measure performance of the "business processes" of the enterprise.
- Adopt a problem-solving and corrective action process.
- Obtain and sustain top management commitment.

The philosophy of continuous improvement has two objectives:

- Provide the tools, techniques, education, and management required for continuous quality and productivity improvement.
- Allow everyone to work together as a team to achieve improvements in quality and productivity.

Successful implementation of a TQM program that ensures continuous improvement must focus on taking a technical journey and a behavioral journey.

The technical journey addresses the specific disciplines and methodologies of the business activity. The behavioral journey addresses the organizational issues, human resource development concerns, and management of the technical activity.

To ensure success of the behavioral journey and the eventual effectiveness of the technical journey, organizations need to institutionalize the management of change. To institutionalize the management of change is to deal with the culture of the organization. To address such issues, *cultural change committees* need to be formed to handle issues relating to

- Management
- Measurement
- Education
- Employee involvement

These committees, working separately and together, create the *environment for success* of the entire TQM effort. They are comprised of mid-level managers responsible for the overall supervision of the business activity.

Since, according to Deming, 85 percent of quality problems lie within the realm of management control, it is imperative that these committees be formed and empowered to function as an extension of executive management.

By focusing the TQM effort on continuous improvement, the following can be expected:

- Communications become more effective.

- Relationships between customers and providers are improved.

- Problems are anticipated and many are eliminated.

- Wasted time and effort are reduced and productive time increased.

Detailed Discussion

Recognizing the Need to Improve

In a general sense the recognition of the need to improve quality centers on trying to sensitize people to the fact that commonly expressed levels of performance, while seeming to be high, may be completely unacceptable when viewed from the perspective of the customer. The following examples are often used as an illustration of what 99.9 percent can really translate to if you are on the receiving end.

- At least 20,000 wrong drug prescriptions each year

- More than 15,000 newborn babies dropped by doctors or nurses each year

- Unsafe drinking water almost one hour each month

- Two short or long landings at major airports each day

- Nearly 500 incorrect surgical operations per week

- 16,000 lost articles of mail per hour

In chapter 3 we will be specific about the need for improving quality in IS; in the meantime, in relation to the previous examples, it would be interesting to know how many have their origin in poor quality information delivered by automated systems.

The second major reason for embracing TQM is the need to be able to *adapt to change*. As we shall see in the remainder of this chapter, TQM provides an excellent forum not only to adapt to change, but to anticipate change as well. This means the ability to respond to changing markets, technology, and competition, and the impact these changes may have on the social structure, revenues, and profitability of a company. By using TQM mechanisms to anticipate change, the opportunities presented by such change can also be explored and potential problems identified and mitigated. TQM utilized in this way becomes an integral part of corporate risk management and strategic planning programs.

Meeting Requirements by Focusing on the Customer

This principle of TQM incorporates the concept of the customer. The objective is to *establish a common understanding of quality with your customer.*

The critical nature of this common understanding of quality should be clear. Without it, meeting the customer's expectation becomes a crapshoot.

The meeting of customer requirements, then, must first and foremost concentrate on the available definitions of quality. Given the product or service to be delivered, how will the customer judge quality?

There are five generally accepted working definitions of *quality* that should be considered:

- *Transcendent:* You *know* what it is, but it cannot be precisely defined. We *know* by comparison.

- *Product-based:* Precise measurement of some attribute—the more of the attribute, the higher the quality. *Higher quality equals higher cost.*

- *User-based:* Highly subjective, since quality is the degree to which specific product satisfies the wants of a specific consumer.

- *Manufacturing-based:* Quality means conformance to a stated and documented requirement. Quality is the degree to which a specific product or service conforms to a specification.

- *Value-based:* Quality is perceived and discussed in relation to a price. How much excellence can you afford?

Agreeing on which definition prevails is the important first step. This agreement will determine what the developer of the goods or service has to live with and how goods and services will be judged by the customer. For example,

- Your customers know what quality is when they see it versus agreed-upon acceptance criteria.
- Higher quality versus higher cost.
- Customer wants versus customer needs.
- Conformance to specification versus shifting expectations of the customer.
- Quality versus value (affordable excellence).

In chapter 3 we will explore how critical this mutual agreement on definition can become and the many ways it may be expressed and measured.

Meeting customer requirements demands that we frame our business actions in the new paradigm of the customer-provider-customer relationship. *Everyone is someone's provider, and everyone is someone's customer.* This new framework includes all people we come into contact with, both inside and outside the enterprise (Figure 2.1).

While meeting the requirements of the external customer pays the bills, sensitivity to the internal customer determines the effectiveness and efficiency with which the external customer is satisfied. Given an understanding of the external customer's requirements, meeting them in an economically efficient manner is the work of dealing with the requirements of the internal customers.

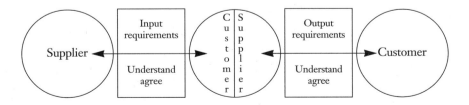

Source: Adapted from J. Michael Crouch, *An Ounce of Application Is Worth a Ton of Abstraction* (Greensboro, N.C.: LEADS Corporation, 1992): 6.

Figure 2.1. Each job (your job).

In a general sense the term *customer* seems rather clear. But for the IS department, such is not the case. While the IS term for customer, *user*, seems straightforward, users actually represent many different organizational interests that must be represented in the definition, design, and acceptance of an information system or service. This existence of multiple customers poses special problems when attempting to meet customer requirements. More on this is discussed in chapter 3.

Error-Free Work or Do Right Things Right the First Time (DRTRFT)

DRTRFT is viewed by some as the *mantra* of TQM. It sets the objective for a continuous improvement effort and is the motivating reason for all TQM activities.

At first glance DRTRFT seems to be a clever statement of *do good and avoid evil*. It smacks of *motherhood, the flag, and apple pie*. It will inevitably provoke derision and be compared to zero defects, management by objectives, zero-based budgeting, quality circles, and other recent doctrines that have tried to revolutionize the way we do business. Blunting such knee-jerk criticism becomes an exercise in persuasion!

To properly define what DRTRFT really means, one must first analyze the statement:

Do right things	=	Performing the requirements definition process correctly.
	=	Obtaining requirements from all appropriate customers.
	=	Reaching agreement with customers on how quality will be defined and measured.
Right the first time	=	Work processes used to satisfy requirements are technically correct, efficient, and cost-effective.
	=	Efficient—working well with little waste.
	=	Effective—producing the desired results.

If DRTRFT were split into a requirements definition phase (DRT), and a construction and delivery phase (RFT), alternatives to DRTRFT can be postulated. For example,

Do Wrong Things Right the First Time (DWTRFT)

Performing an analysis similar to the preceding one would indicate that with DWTRFT there is a problem with our requirements definition process and a failure to reach agreement on what quality means to the customer and how it will be measured.

It matters little that we can construct the product efficiently; it does not meet the customer's requirements—it may even be considered a quality product—but it is the *wrong product*. For example, you order a quarter-pound hamburger with cheese but get a chicken fillet. In the drive-thru, of course, no simple exchange is possible. No doubt it is a quality chicken fillet, but it is not what you ordered. Your impression of service quality goes down.

Do Right Things Wrong the First Time (DRTWFT)

This version indicates difficulty in the construction and delivery of the product or service to specification. There is a clear requirements statement. The specifications include an understanding of how the quality of the product or service will be measured. *We just cannot deliver.* When and if we do deliver, the cost far exceeds our estimate because we had to do the job more than once. The classic example is probably the automobile recall. Detroit may indeed spend several years in designing and specifying the requirements of a new car, but flaws in the construction phase result in costly recalls and tarnishes customer opinion of the company.

Do Wrong Things Wrong the First Time (DWTWFT)

This probably is like a joke to most people. After all, how often could you get the requirement wrong, the specifications for quality wrong, and the construction wrong? Maybe after reflection, DWTWFT explains the extremely low customer satisfaction indicated in Figure 1.1 (on page 2). What else but a bad case of DWTWFT could explain it?

What is error-free work and what constitutes an error-free mindset? First, error-free work is not a motivation program; it is not a ploy to get everyone to do better and work harder. Error-free work does not concentrate on the individual worker. Error-free work

- Asks what went wrong, not who did it
- Recognizes that it is always cheaper to DRTRFT
- Believes every error has causes that can be identified and eliminated
- Organizes and plans every job with the goal of error-free work
- Plans measurable improvement toward the goal of error-free work

Without the right culture (acceptance of what is wrong), you cannot obtain answers to the question, *What went wrong?*

Managing by Prevention

The fourth principle of TQM is to manage by prevention. This is the process by which error-free work is planned.

In Figure 2.2. the past/present curve illustrates the way we have historically done things: very little upfront planning/prevention, while letting the customer act as the final inspector. Notice the similarity between Figure 2.2, which applies to all work processes, and Figure 1.4 (on page 8), which applies to the correction of errors in IS projects. Both figures proceed to identify a common problem to which advanced planning and preventive thinking offer solutions.

In both cases, *managing by prevention* will create a future curve (Figure 2.2) where time is allowed and expected to be spent up-front to practice prevention. This reduces the effort spent, after the customer receives the service or product, in trying to make things *right!* It also eliminates the primary cause of poor quality perceptions customers develop about an organization.

One of the major challenges of managing by prevention is the cultural impact it will have on the typical organization. This principle of TQM questions how projects are planned, how contract terms and agreements are managed, and how management and employees are rewarded.

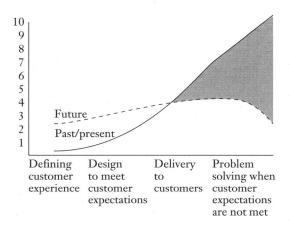

Source: Reprinted with permission from J. Michael Crouch, LEADS Corporation.

Figure 2.2. Effort by activity.

If the management style is reactive in nature, this will be reflected in the way the project is managed. If corporate advanced planning is not the norm, projects will follow suit. If project *due dates* are driven by unrealistic expectations, politics, or other factors, the time necessary to practice preventive management will undoubtedly be reduced. After all, the due date has already been set; you cannot waste time analyzing the project—just build it and deliver it. This, of course, perpetuates the reality of Figures 1.4 and 2.2.

Often, contractual arrangements do not encourage advance planning. Certain contracts, for example, allow the complexity and uncertainty of a task to be passed on to the customer and rewards little or no preventive thinking and poor planning. The cost estimates for such contracts are not going to be as well thought out as in the case where a product is expected for a fixed price. Such cost estimates often tend to *lowball* in order to get a *foot in the door.*

The issue of contract language also has a profound effect. It is possible to have contract terms negate the preventive management philosophy of a TQM effort. If it is assured, in contract language, that I will be able to pass complexity and uncertainty onto the customer, there is little incentive to take a preventive management approach. It does not matter how well we practice preventive thinking and advanced planning, we will get paid anyway because payment for the project occurs at various predetermined points. The practice of levying penalties for nonperformance may satisfy the contracting official, but it is of little practical use to the customer who still has to get a job accomplished.

In the final analysis contracts that we *let* and contracts that we *obtain* should support, not contradict, the TQM principle of preventive management we are trying to foster in our organization.

The last cultural aspect of the organization that preventive management brings into question deals with how and for what employees rewarded. This raises the question of who gets rewarded—planners and preventive thinkers or firefighters. Remember, people do what they are rewarded for.

Does the manager who practices error prevention and who plans a project with honest resource estimates and enforces standards get rewarded for such practices, or do such attempts at rational management get slighted as the latest project in crisis gets resolved by the *fire fighter?* A fire fighter who should have been practicing prevention all along.

As a rule, does the reward and incentives system promote the mentality of catching problems at the end regardless of cost, or the preventive mentality? Notice that the main components of prevention are to *anticipate, plan,* and *act;* the fire fighter, through inspection, tends to solve the same problems over and over again on project after project. In fact it is sometimes whispered that such people, if continuously rewarded, often create or purposely overlook problems so that they may assume the savior role late in the project's life. Cultural change committees must work hard and steadily to overcome such influences.

Identify and Measure Cost of Quality

Cost of quality, the fifth principle of TQM, is critical for the long-term success of the total effort. While it has been said that *quality is free,* this could only be true in an environment where the practices of TQM are already standard business practice. Most organizations are not there yet, and so there will be certain ramp-up costs associated with institutionalizing TQM principles and practices. *Identifying and monitoring the cost of quality allows the initial cost of the ramp-up to be offset by actual benefits.* Identifying and monitoring the cost of quality also allows us to specify the areas of the business process needing attention through the problem-solving program.

One way to express this is through an examination of Figure 2.2 (on page 24). The shaded area illustrates that the problem-solving activities necessary to meet customer expectations are a form of *waste* and therefore represent lost resources and profit. It is a loss due to

- Right things done wrong
- Wrong things done right
- Wrong things done wrong

These are the *negative* costs of quality, and it is not uncommon for such waste to represent more than 25 percent of revenues or budget. That is, a 25 percent improvement can be made in the financial picture of the enterprise by just eliminating waste. In the private sector this can be profit or investments for future competitiveness. In the government sector a 25 percent improvement provides resources to meet new legislative mandates, cut into backlogs, or improve service to the public.

As mentioned earlier, however, quality does require some expenditure of resources, but for preventive purposes! These are the *positive* costs of quality. While not reflecting all of the necessary expenditures, Figure 2.2 indicates those costs required for preventive thinking and advanced planning. This increase is illustrated by the raised future line over the past/present line. Other positive costs are training and tools to better equip personnel to build quality the first time.

We are really dealing with a reallocation of resources from the shaded or waste area to the front-end definition and design phases where training, thinking, and planning prevent problems. These up-front increases in effort will result in sizeable reductions in the shaded or waste area since the cost to solve and fix problems, after a product or service has been delivered to a customer, is much greater than preventing problems in the first place. The impact of so-called intangible costs, such as loss of reputation, loss of credibility, and customer dissatisfaction, will also be reduced. We are spared the additional costs associated with resolving problems with products already in the customer's hands.

Finally, since product and service quality is our best advertisement, we are spared that portion of continuing expenses required to just hold our market share. Since repeat business with satisfied, existing customers is more likely, we can spend our marketing dollars to expand the business to new customers, rather than on repairing damaged relations with old customers.

Measure Performance of the Business Process

The objective of this principle of a TQM program is to gather and analyze data to support corrective actions and improvements to business processes. As a tool, measurement is vital if an organization is to know how its business is doing. Measurement of *cost of quality*, for example, helps us understand what it really costs to provide customers with a quality product or service. There is, however, great fear and trepidation at the thought of measuring anything that could reflect adversely on individuals, the group, or management of the group.

For this reason it is imperative that measurement activities not be perceived as the basis for adverse employee actions. Since candor in measurement (especially when reporting errors) is all important, this point cannot be overemphasized. In the rare case (15 percent or less according to Deming) where an employee appears to have made an error, closer examination will probably reveal problems with the training process, the supervision process, or the quality review process.

Once the process orientation of measurement is made evident to the employees, real candor in reporting will result. Truthfulness in measurement will reveal the actual workings of business processes and serve as the basis for problem-solving and corrective action decisions.

What and how to measure should be determined by the affected work group (that is, what errors will be measured). Measurements must be objective; you must be able to count occurrences of not meeting the requirement or the deviations from a standard. Measurements must be used positively to improve the work process, not to punish!

Finally, measurements are used to determine where we have been, where we are going, and how we are doing. Measurement allows management to take a snapshot of the business process at any point in time and monitor the pulse of customer satisfaction.

Adopt a Problem-Solving and Corrective Action Process

The purpose of this principle of a TQM program is to institutionalize problem solving such that corrective actions actually solve problems more than once. The purpose, through analysis, is to get to the *root cause* of problems and implement corrective actions aimed at that root cause and not just symptoms.

Too often, problem solving has been viewed as those corrective actions taken to get a troubled product out the door! This type of activity is *rework*, not problem solving, and is a major contributor to waste.

Traditionally, problem solving does not occur until we are in a crisis of some sort and cannot tolerate the pain any longer. We then hurriedly take some correction action aimed, not at the problem, but at the symptoms. Then it's back to work until the next crisis occurs. Nothing has changed. The workprocess and conditions that created the problem have not been addressed, so the same or similar problems are likely to recur. Furthermore, since we have not uncovered the underlying causes and analyzed them, we are unable to devise any *early warning systems* to keep management informed of developing future problems.

Another major benefit of a problem-solving process is the ability to identify, through impact analysis, the ripple effect that even a seemingly minor problem can have on other components of the enterprise. This impact, when cost of quality is calculated at each organizational point where the impact is felt, can be much larger than originally thought. The domino effect of quality problems in one workprocess affects the customer of that workprocess output, and the next and the next, as each subsequent customer has to undertake corrective cleanup work to make the work-product usable. This can be especially insidious where information systems are concerned because a lack of information quality is not readily apparent. Much is accepted as fact simply because the *computer says so!*

But how can problems in a workprocess be identified short of a crisis or a complaining customer? In a preventive vein the people within the process can ask, *What keeps me from doing my job* right the first time? While some of these problems can be handled by the local supervisor, many will be problems that are beyond control of local management. Problems that involve other departments become more difficult to address. Such problems require visibility and management commitment to solve. Interpersonal communications present the major hurdle. Use of a formal problem-solving process will gain everyone's attention and cooperation to solve such problems.

Such a process, properly conducted, can answer the following questions:

- What is the problem?

  —Not people-oriented

  —No finger-pointing

- Where is the problem found?
- When did it happen?
- How big is it? What is the ripple effect or impact on subsequent customers? What is it costing?
- Is it growing?
- How will we know when it is solved?

The last question forces the identification of *measures* and the early warning indicators necessary to monitor for problem recurrence.

The most common group technique used for problem solving is *brainstorming*. Reverse brainstorming is sometimes used for problem prevention. Reverse brainstorming takes a product, service, or process that appears to be satisfactory and asks the question, *What could we do that would result in lowered quality and/or productivity?*

Brainstorming assists teams in identifying elements of the problem or project potential problems. Group dynamics is used to build teamwork. Members of the team will have increased feelings of control over the job, and, importantly, it builds ownership of derived solutions and their implementation.

Since solutions may require the expenditures of resources, it is necessary to identify all current categories of waste and calculate a reasonable *cost of quality* for the problem, including any ripple effect impacting other internal customers.

In some implementations of problem solving the team will perform a roadblock analysis, and attempt to mitigate such roadblocks in the plan for corrective action implementation.

Obtain and Sustain Top Management Commitment

Was there ever an organizational improvement initiative that did not claim to require top management support to be successful? On the other hand, when such initiatives fail, it is said that they lacked top management support. This is true of TQM as well, but there are several reasons why it is easier to obtain and sustain this level of support with TQM.

First, TQM is not a separate activity to be laminated onto existing management practices. TQM simply provides a focus of *continuous improvement* and *prevention* to the existing management process.

Both of these concepts support the goal of DRTRFT, which in turn results in satisfied customers and efficient use of resources. *What management would not support these objectives?* Furthermore, TQM provides top management with a new perspective through which all organizational activity and initiatives can be viewed. Simply put, any business activity, current or planned, should be able to show a positive relationship to the following three questions:

- What will the activity do to improve the quality of our products or services?

- If the activity is not helping our customer reach their quality goals, why are we doing it?

- If the activity is not helping to reduce our cost of quality, why are we doing it?

Consistent use of these three questions can go farther to indicate management's commitment to quality than almost any other action. It forces all organizational elements to focus and articulate the quality relationship of all its activities, plans, acquisitions, and so on. It actually forces a sort of *corporate quality impact analysis.*

In addition to these three questions, top management commitment is demonstrated by the actions management takes to change the organizational culture and create an environment within which the practices of TQM can flourish. This is the behavioral journey without which the technical journey cannot succeed.

Institutionalizing the Management of Change

The purpose of cultural change committees is to create an environment for success and to convey continuing top management commitment, support, and interest. There should be committees to address at least four major areas:

- Management
- Measurement
- Education
- Employee involvement

These committees should be staffed by mid-level managers, perhaps even those most resistant to change. Each committee performs the following functions and reports to top management (that is, a steering committee).

Management Committee

This committee seeks out actions, which employees want to see and hear, that support the quality improvement process and make sure there is a flow of these actions. The committee is empowered to make sure that all quality-oriented communications are clearly conveyed to all employees. It is responsible for scheduling and organizing appropriate events to reinforce participation and teamwork.

Measurement Committee

The measurement committee determines areas, especially at senior levels of the enterprise, for measurement. These areas include high-level indicators dealing with external customers and their degree of satisfaction with the enterprise. Customer surveys are frequently used to measure such satisfaction. Internal measurement of workprocesses can be influenced by the measurements this committee determines are important to external customers.

Education Committee

This committee is responsible for arranging TQM education to ensure knowledgeable employee implementation of quality practices, such as preventive thinking and problem solving. This committee may also assume responsibility for ensuring that training in core business knowledge and skills is available and consistent with the business and technical direction of the organization.

Employee Involvement Committee

This committee is responsible for defining how the problem-solving process will work. They design a tailored procedure for the organization. The committee is also responsible for defining and implementing an employee/team recognition program that rewards prevention as opposed to fire fighting.

Summary and Conclusions

Chapter 2 has endeavored to impart a working knowledge of the generic principles of TQM. It has been based on the extensive experience of the LEADS Corporation and the author's experience in attempting to apply these generic elements to information technology groups. In chapter 3 we will discuss those experiences and explore the impact TQM implementation can have on the rest of the enterprise.

3 TQM for the IS Department

Introduction

Based on the generic description of TQM presented in the previous chapter, it is the intent here to explore the application of TQM to the business of IS. The next four chapters will endeavor to deal with the following questions and issues:

- How important is a TQM initiative in the IS department to the rest of the enterprise?
- How does the business of IS relate to the thought process and activities required of a TQM continuous-improvement program?
- How difficult would it be to initiate a TQM effort in the IS department?
- What would such an effort really *buy* the rest of the enterprise?

Chapter 7 will then discuss a possible TQM implementation and structure, and chapter 8 will project a future where the relationship of the IS department to other business units has been transformed around the commonly understood language, goals, and objectives of quality and continuous improvement.

The Business of IS

Any application of TQM presupposes a clear understanding of the business in which we are engaged. To understand the business of information services, we must discuss the nature and role of information in the management of organizations that are conducting commercial activities or carrying out government mandates.

According to Webster:[11]

- *Information*—knowledge obtained from investigation, study, or instruction

- *System*—a set or arrangement of things so related or connected as to form a unity

- *Process*—a method of doing something, generally involving a number of steps or operations

Based on these definitions information systems can be viewed as an arrangement of units (that is, processes) that provide knowledge obtained from investigation, study, or instruction.

Therefore, the business of IS is to design, construct, operate, and maintain information systems. The IS function may be centralized or decentralized and dispersed. This dispersion does not change the functions to be performed nor does it reduce the level of knowledge and skill required to carry out the service of developing and delivering systems.

Simply put, the business of IS is to provide customers with quality information through systems and processes that have integrity (reliability) (Figure 3.1). What does this mean?

Quality Information

In a practical sense and within the modern automated enterprise, what is the role of information? Information is a medium through which knowledge of the condition status of organizational assets and resources is conveyed to management. Information representing the condition and status of personnel, capital, and materials being utilized to carry out the purpose of the enterprise allows decision makers to manage these resources and assets effectively and efficiently. Information must convey the reality of resource usage so that well-founded decisions can be made concerning future resource needs and their allocation.

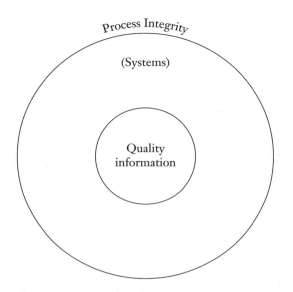

Figure 3.1. Process integrity.

If the status information representing any resource is *inaccurate* or otherwise *misleading*, the success rate of resultant decisions using that information will suffer. If information concerning any one resource is misleading, it may prove difficult to manage even that one resource. If the misleading nature of the information is known, management can make allowance and compensate for it during the decision process. If, on the other hand, the misleading nature of the information is unknown, its use will certainly contribute to poorer decisions. The latter case is especially insidious since the decision maker places trust in the information when trust is not warranted.

Notice that this role of information, as representing reality, does not change with regard to the type of decision being made. It is as valid for a decision regarding the balancing of your checking account as it is for a *real-time* automated action (decision) taken by a process control application during a machine tooling job. In both cases misleading information will result in less-than-optimal decisions or actions taking place.

From this realization of the importance of information to the enterprise, the following basic tenets of information resource management have evolved:

- Information is a management resource and organizational asset on a par with personnel, money, buildings, equipment, know-how, reputation, and credibility.

- Effective and efficient management of other corporate resources and assets is impossible if information does not present the accurate *status* and *condition* of those resources.

- Each manager's responsibility for information is no less than for any other resource or asset within his or her domain.

- Decisions concerning information activities rank in significance and priority with decisions on other major strategies, plans, and actions.

But are these concepts new? Wouldn't these basic tenets have been just as valid 100 years ago? Why has their importance only recently surfaced?

No, there is nothing new! Yes, these tenets were equally valid 100 years ago or even 1000 years ago! Why the recent emergence and importance?

Technology has changed the way in which information is brought to decision makers. Computing and communicating technologies have dramatically expanded the range of observation for the decision maker. Before the technological advances of the last hundred years, observation was limited to the five senses; assignment of meaning to those observations was generally limited to the intelligence, training, and experience of the observer; and communication was limited to the speed of a fast horse.

Students of military history will immediately recognize these as the limiting factors of command and control before the advent of twentieth century technologies. At the Battle of Gettysburg, for example, it has long been noted that the effectiveness of the Confederate forces was severely hampered by a lack of intelligence regarding Union troop movements. This lack of information was due to the fact that General Robert E. Lee lost his *eyes and ears* and much of his communications capability due to the absence of Jeb Stuart and his cavalry.

Today technology automates the activities of observing and sensing, partially automates the assignment of meaning to those observations, and communicates the resultant information to human beings for decisions or directly to electromechanical mechanisms to activate some device, such as a wing deicing unit.

Wherever the human element has been bypassed, the function has either been eliminated or is being executed by some analog or binary device. In such cases the function now being performed must be the result of extremely detailed and precise instructions.

These instructions (software) must be thoughtfully defined, designed, developed, and tested, since all or part of the ability of humans to perceive subtle distinctions and variations in data and processing may have been eliminated.

The manager of today most often does not deal with the real world through direct observation. The modern manager deals with a depiction of the real world presented through readouts, graphics, reports, models, and spreadsheets. If these depictions are not reliable, the manager's perception of the real world will be flawed and distorted.

If the information system is also expected to *manipulate* such data, search for trends and patterns, and impart meaning (create information), without human intervention the real-world perception can become even more flawed. Now, communicate this flawed information to a customer for immediate use in carrying some business-related activity and watch trust in the system and confidence in the IS department disintegrate!

Process (Systems) Integrity

Figure 3.1 illustrates quality information as nested within process and systems integrity. This indeed is the relationship since information systems and processes either maintain and add value to information or destroy the representativeness and value of information. The arrangement of processing units can either function to deliver good quality information or poor quality misinformation to the customer.

Since quality information is delivered to customers through processes and systems that are reliable, it is clear that the very reason for the existence of an IS department is to build such systems!

How successful is the typical IS department at delivering reliable information systems/processes that provide quality information? These questions were raised and answered in chapter 1 as we explored the perceptions of the IS department. It is only important here to state, and then to continuously reinforce, the *absolute importance* of the IS department and its work-products to the enterprise as a whole! These work-products touch all aspects of the modern enterprise and, in many cases, society as a whole.

The Linchpin Phenomenon Revisited

While the work-products of other business units have a well-understood customer exposure, it seems that the exposure of IS work-products is both more extensive and critical than commonly perceived. The linchpin phenomenon, discussed in chapter 1, is revisited here because it appears that this phenomenon may be at the center of some of the criticism that is now being leveled at TQM in general.

As described by various TQM facilitators, it appears that after the obvious and easy quality improvements have been made, TQM progress begins to slow. It seems that to make the next level of improvement, the business process itself must be *redesigned*. But it is automated, which means that IS involvement is required if meaningful redesign is to take place. But where is the IS department? Statistics show that 70 percent to 80 percent of IS resources are fully employed in just maintaining current systems, that is, keeping them up and making minor enhancements. Also, since few IS departments have really begun an active pursuit of TQM, yet another language barrier is being erected between IS and their customers. This time it is the language of quality and continuous improvement.

It is becoming evident that unless and until the IS department becomes active in TQM and in the quality initiatives of its customers, the next level of improvement (business process redesign) will be a long time coming. For those readers who just thought *outsource the business redesign*, remember that you need the goodwill and cooperation of the IS department, as maintainers of the current systems, to successfully outsource any development or redesign project.

Figure 3.2 depicts the relationship between internal IS department workprocesses (that is, the way IS builds information systems) and the customer's workprocess (the systems built by IS).

Until TQM and the continuous improvement philosophy is brought to bear on the internal world of IS, it is doubtful that a positive influence can be projected toward the customer's work processes. Yet it is the customer's work processes and the goods and services from those processes that determine the quality/productivity profile of the enterprise and subsequent success or failure with customers in the marketplace.

Improving the Quality of IS Department Work Products: An Application of TQM to the Systems Development Process (SDP)

By way of review, TQM and the philosophy of continuous improvement focus on the workprocess, not the product. The rationale is that if the process is improved, the quality of the product will improve. Establishing

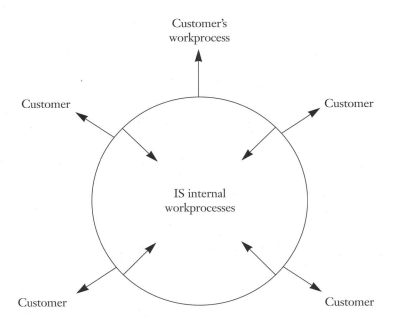

Figure 3.2. IS manager's TQM sphere of influence.

mechanisms to continuously monitor the process, prevent or identify problems, and take corrective actions will improve the products of the process.

For the IS department then, application of TQM means examining the *process* by which we manage and develop information systems and processes for our customers.

No, that was not a stutter! *TQM means examining the process the IS department uses to build processes!*

As with any application of TQM, if the process by which we produce our product (that is, quality information and reliable systems) is flawed, then the product will be flawed. This is truly a situation where *one must remove the spectacles to see them clearly.* So what are the spectacles through which the IS department views the world? What is the process by which we build systems?

The answer should surprise no one; the process is called the *systems development process* (SDP). In its many variations it is the systematic and analytic process by which

- Development efforts are managed

- Requirements are analyzed, defined, and specified

- Solutions are explored and designed

- Programs are coded, databases built, and equipment and networks procured

- System components are arranged and tested

- Systems are accepted for use by the customer

There are many models of the SDP, such as the following:

- Traditional continuum or waterfall model

- Cyclic or interactive model

- Operational models

- Spiral model

Some of these versions have strict methodologies, some are more flexible. Some promote the concurrent execution of certain process steps. All versions attempt to impose a discipline on the business of building information systems. All are valid. And, in the heat of battle, all are generally ignored, circumvented, or incompletely applied.

A classic cartoon says it best. The supervisor is pictured about to leave a room of computer programmers. His instructions, "You all begin coding I'll go see what they want." In other words, start building a solution before we have even defined the problem.

An inside joke among IS department personnel is the fact that they all admit to having some version of an SDP in their work group. Some of these versions are very expensive methodologies supported by automated tools. Insiders will also generally admit that they do not use or enforce the use of the SDP.

Why is this the case? If the insider is to be believed (go ask someone), then TQM-like techniques for process improvements are already available, but they are being rejected by the culture of the IS department. Or is there another problem?

While cultural rejection does occur, there are other more likely reasons for the failure to adhere to the SDP discipline when building information systems. First, many people in IS do not really understand the SDP—why, how, and when to use it. Go to any computer bookstore and examine the table of contents of almost any book dealing with your PC, favorite spreadsheet, a language you would like to learn, or a database package. In the vast majority of cases nothing will be presented on the SDP. Nothing will be discussed about the sequence of analysis steps required to solve an information processing problem. Nothing will be presented on how to work with customers to solve their business information problem—to identify their information requirements. The only type of problem solving discussed deals with the PC itself (hardware and operating system) and debugging language statements. In other words, problem solving revolves around making the hardware and software platform work and not how to solve the business problem of the customer.

Second, many individuals have not been trained in the use of the SDP. Often too little money is programmed for adequate training after the methodology and support tools have been purchased and installed. Recent estimates by Department of Defense officials suggest that for every $1 spent on SDP methodologies and support tools, $4 needs to be spent on training and technology transfer.

Third, who has the time to learn and apply even the most useful techniques when one is in constant crisis? It has long been recognized that a catch-22 situation exists in many IS departments: *There is no time to do it right, but there is always time to do it again. We are too busy fixing yesterday's problem to prevent tomorrow's.*

There is another reason that most IS people can relate to—the discipline of the SDP demands great understanding and cooperation on the part of the customer. *The SDP, as a problem-solving/analytic process, requires intimate understanding of the business process on the part of the customer if an adequate automated specification is to be defined that can guide the construction and delivery of the system.*

In the experience of many the SDP has been tried and found wanting. The failures seem to fall into three areas:

- Inability of the IS department to adequately manage the environment in which the SDP must function

- Failure to generate accurate requirements describing the information system to be built

- Difficulty in using available technology and executing the construction and delivery phases of the SDP

Chapters 4, 5, and 6 will address these areas. We will see how the application of TQM principles can greatly improve the probability of successfully negotiating the SDP.

4 TQM and Management of the SDP I: Creating the Environment for Success

Introduction

How would the application of TQM and its philosophy and principles affect the process of defining, constructing, and delivering information systems? How would an IS department proceed to improve the quality of its services? Since we have identified the central work process of IS to be the SDP, let us explore the impact of the TQM principles from chapter 2 on that work process.

For ease of presentation let us apply *DRTRFT* to a simple version of the SDP. We can assign *DRT* to the early requirements definition phases of the SDP and *RFT* to the construction and delivery phases.

Figure 4.1 illustrates the major SDP phases in light of DRTRFT. It also shows *quality assurance* activities that must be performed if DRTRFT is to be achieved. Viewed this way, the SDP appears as a fully TQM-compatible mechanism in which the principles of TQM and the philosophy of continuous improvement can be implemented. *After all, no one consciously begins a development effort with the intention of building a poor system.*

Requirements definition		Systems construction and delivery
DRT		RFT
Requirements are clear, concise, and measurable.		SDP execution for meeting requirements is effective and efficient.
Quality assurance }	Validate the requirement!	Validate and verify that development is sound and proper. Test throughout!

Figure 4.1. SDP.

Preventive Thinking Prior to SDP Initiation

Preventive thinking prior to beginning a project and attempting to follow the SDP means identifying potential problems that could hinder successful completion of the requirements definition, construction, and delivery of the system. In a sense this analysis assigns a degree of complexity to the system to be built and determines identifiable conditions that often surround a development effort. Table 4.1 lists conditions that commonly contribute to a high-risk development effort, one that is likely to result in poor quality systems and service.

> Failure to anticipate and fully understand the implication of each of these conditions, manage them effectively, and communicate their impact to executive management is a fundamental cause of system development failure.[12]

These conditions represent *structural management problems* that result in *doing it wrong*. In other words, even with a complete, clear, and concise definition of the IS requirement, including measurable quality attributes and performance metrics, the IS department will be unable to construct and deliver a quality information product. This is because the existence of such structural management problems exerts an overwhelmingly negative influence on the ability to construct and deliver the system. *Such structural problems make RFT impossible!*

- Lack of top management commitment
- Inadequate planning and budgeting
- Abandonment of the plan
- Lack of trained personnel
- Inexperienced project managers
- Flawed technical approach
- Failure to anticipate change
- High turnover in personnel
- Inadequate documentation
- Unrealistic cost estimates
- Failure to manage and enforce the SDP
- Nonquality work by support vendors
- Questionable reliability of support vendors

Table 4.1. Structural management problems.

These structural management problems depict historical and well-documented conditions adversely affecting the workprocesses of the IS department. *They represent the starting point for an internal TQM program. They must be addressed if the customer perceptions of chapter 1 are to be changed and if the IS department ever hopes to contribute positively to the customer's quality and productivity goals.* They must be addressed by identifying both behavioral and technical changes in the way IS conducts its business.

The following centers on how TQM implementation within the IS department can assist managers in identifying and mapping solutions to many of these structural management problems.

Recognition of the Need for Improvement

For the sake of variety let us go at this in reverse. While conventional brainstorming is effective once a problem has been identified, *reverse brainstorming* assists in coming to grips with the existence and reality of a problem. The problem of nonquality IS products is so pervasive, the cost of making systems work so high, late delivery so acceptable, and customer dissatisfaction so commonplace, that many IS personnel and customers know of no other way for their business to be conducted. Recalling our earlier inside joke concerning the fact that most IS personnel admit to having a version of the SDP, but that it is not followed or enforced, the same insider would snicker at the list in Table 4.1 and ask, *So what else is new?* By reverse brainstorming perhaps we can get the attention of these insiders. Remember the prerequisite to successful TQM implementation is an understanding of and commitment to the need for change.

Identifying Structural Management Problems

For our reverse brainstorming let us assume a workplace in which IS quality products are the norm, customers are satisfied, projects are completed on time and under budget, our credibility is high, all employees are self-fulfilled, no one is threatening outsourcing, all documentation is complete, and the CIO just received the team player of the year award from the CEO. Reverse brainstorming begins by asking, *How can we, in the IS department, screw up this nirvana? What can we do to get ourselves cast out of the garden?* People love to reverse brainstorm. It is like a game, a game that is nonthreatening and, therefore, enjoyable.

With little effort the participants will begin to identify actions they could take that would ruin the wonderful working environment of the scenario. For example, the group could do the following:

- Make system construction and delivery promises that are politically pleasing, but unsound.
- Not require comprehensive customer participation in requirements definition and validation in order to speed up the project.
- Not require work estimates to be generated at the lowest possible organizational level.
- Not require a peer or independent evaluation of technical solutions for meeting customer requirements.

- Allow design solutions to be unduly influenced by a favorite vendor.
- Not require complete documentation for each phase of the project.
- Not enforce the discipline of structured techniques.
- Not keep track of resource utilization against estimates.
- Not perform periodic assessments of those technologies that are central to development efforts.
- Reduce personnel costs by recruiting less qualified people.
- Provide less visible and less understood career paths within the IS department.
- Fail to equip technical personnel moving into management by cutting all related training.
- Rely solely on OJT (on-the-job training) for new hires.
- Reorganize to create more or higher graded positions for a few.
- Reorganize to create more lower graded positions for the many.
- Reduce all testing and talk the customer into becoming your BETA tester.
- Stop requiring quality products from suppliers.
- Let the SDP become an inside joke.

At some point, the group participants will begin to realize that they are describing many of the actual conditions under which they are now operating. Eyes will begin to open!

There are other approaches for generating the same results. It is common to obtain a list of structural management problems by directly addressing the implementation of some future initiative. For example, the IS department may have been directed to prepare for a *fee for service* environment. In this instance a TQM facilitation could begin by having the management group address *inhibitors* to being successful in a fee for service environment. This approach is preventive thinking in nature and results in plans for TQM initiatives that reduce the future risk of failure and improve day-to-day activity.

An even more direct method is to ask, *What problems do we in the IS department have in delivering quality information services to our customers?* This latter approach may put some people off and make them cautious about being critical of others in the group. More commonly, the group will use it as a forum to identify why all the problems lie outside the group and with the customer or some bureaucracy. Mysterious *theys* and *thems* are referred to. In any case it is easy to use this approach to generate a list of structural management problems.

From Structural Management Problems to Management Recognition Statements

The list of structural management problems will rarely appear as the clear-cut statements seen in Table 4.1. They will usually be disguised as symptomatic problems. Such symptomatic problems reflect the *crisis* that each manager was facing before entering the room. These symptoms must be reworked into problem statements that reflect the underlying management impediment and allow managers to address them at their level of responsibility.

One of the tenets of TQM is to *solve problems once*, not over and over again, and to solve them at the organizational level closest to the problem. Clearly, the problems in Table 4.1 cannot be solved by employees. Even if they could, they would have to be solved repeatedly because the underlying causes are not being addressed. To rework these symptomatic problems into a form that management can address, we should aggregate and summarize them under the traditional management function categories of

- Planning
- Budgeting
- Organizing
- Staffing
- Directing
- Coordinating

- Controlling
- Reporting

These traditional categories represent the level of responsibility of all managers and the level at which they can solve symptomatic problems. *If the management team does not deal at this level, no one else can!* The management group can argue definitions, but the important point is to begin to deal with the symptomatic problems from a management perspective.

This transition is absolutely necessary if the management team is to ever come out of the day-to-day crises and begin to focus on their management processes and the impact they have on successfully delivering quality services. This transition will make clear Deming's assertion that 85 percent of the quality and productivity problems lie with the management process, and that the vast majority of solutions must begin by addressing these management processes. For our purpose, this also means management of the SDP, since it is the core business process of the IS department. Perhaps a composite example drawn from consulting with actual IS department management teams would be helpful at this point.

After generating lists of symptomatic problems, numbering up to 38 with one group, the problems were aggregated by the IS department managers into the previously discussed management function categories. To illustrate, the following symptomatic problems under the management function of *planning* were gathered:

- Lack of comprehensive IS goals
- Lack of consistent sound analytical studies
- Lack of well-understood and documented estimating techniques
- Lack of coordinated planning
- Lack of consistent priorities
- Lack of consideration for impact on existing work load when tasked
- Annual rather than constant planning

After some overnight reflection and teamwork, the symptomatic problems related to planning were reduced to a simple, high-level management recognition statement.

> The lack of a clear set of goals and objectives leads to poorly understood and uncoordinated planning and results in crisis management.

Now you have a problem that IS department managers should be dealing with instead of putting out fires that were the result of a lack of planning.

One further example from our composite example: Under the management function category of *staffing* the following symptomatic problems were listed.

- Lack of management skills
- Lack of a comprehensive training program for employees
- A mismatch of skills versus work to do
- Serious morale problems throughout the department

After reflection these symptomatic problems were reduced to the following statement:

> The fact that many key positions have not been filled, the difficulties the department has experienced in recruiting qualified candidates, and the lack of training to upgrade management and technical skills are the basic causes of staff deficiencies.

Similar high-level management recognition statements would be generated for each of the remaining management function categories. One may be tempted to think that these examples are extreme. One may ask, *If the managers were not addressing the issues reflected in these management recognition statements, what were they doing?* (They were putting out fires and dealing repeatedly with symptoms of the real problem.) This is the catch-22 situation referred to earlier—this, and the fact that many managers have not been properly prepared to manage and end up doing the technical jobs of their subordinates, rather than the management job they were empowered to do.

From the perspective of the TQM principles and philosophy outlined in chapter 2, a great deal is accomplished by this approach. First, management commitment is demonstrated because TQM has started at the top of the organization. Second, by obtaining management recognition statements centered on management problems, all subsequent TQM activities have a much greater chance of success. Third, the critically important TQM behavioral journey has begun because management has *put itself on notice* and will be taking steps to create an environment for the success of all other TQM initiatives.

To recap, the initial efforts of our TQM initiative must focus on management and any structural problems that are preventing DRTRFT. Without starting at this level, any other involvement by employees will merely result in the same frustration that ended most employee suggestion and quality circle programs of the 1970s and 1980s. Namely, many notable and worthwhile improvement suggestions were made by employees. Since the vast majority of problems lie within the realm of management processes, however, such suggestions were local in scope, could only treat symptoms, and, when they did identify management problems, were seen as threats to the authority and position of managers.

With TQM beginning at the top of the IS department with management process problems, the way is paved for real success at lower levels of the organization. This approach demonstrates top management support for all other TQM activities.

Establishing Ownership of Management Recognition Statements and Developing Corrective Actions

The TQM principles and philosophy described in chapter 2, while often disparaged as just common sense, force recognition of a great truth concerning the realities expressed in management recognition statements. To a greater or lesser degree, these statements indicate that such commonsense principles of product and service delivery are not being followed. Not until improvements are made to these management conditions will meaningful progress be possible in more technical areas.

As we have seen, the organizational mechanisms recommended in chapter 2 for implementing TQM initiatives are as follows:

- Problem-solving and corrective action teams
- Cultural change committees for
  —Management
  —Measurement
  —Education
  —Employee involvement

In most IS departments behavioral change activities can be addressed by the cultural change committees, while technical change activities should be addressed by problem-solving and corrective action teams.

The management recognition statements for each of our management function areas could be tackled through either a cultural change committee, a problem-solving and corrective action team, or both. Whichever route is chosen, ownership for each statement must be established, a set of solutions developed, and implementation assignments made.

Ownership

Management recognition statement ownership can be assigned to an individual team member or to an organizational entity. This assignment affixes responsibility for the successful search for solutions to the problem statement and for monitoring corrective actions.

Determining solutions for the type of issues documented in the management recognition statements is somewhat different than for typical technical process problems identified through TQM workprocess examinations. Solutions to management problems are inexorably tied up in personalities, politics, power, and organizational dynamics, while the typical workprocess problem tends to deal with the mechanics of the work steps themselves.

At management levels it is far more difficult to keep the search for solutions from becoming *finger-pointing* and an exercise in *one-upmanship!*

Rules of Engagement

To prevent such disharmony, a few rules of engagement are needed for the management team as it searches for solutions.

- Members may state their suggested improvement based on what needs to be done, not who did what.

- Members may state how it should be handled, not why it happened. (If it is not known why and how something happened or alternative solutions are not available, a subordinate group can be asked to research the matter.)

- Members must concentrate on what can be done now to prevent future occurrences by taking a workprocess view of the situation.

- Members must talk about what we can do, not what they have done to us or what they are going to do!

- Members are forbidden to use *killer phrases* during any of the discussion, especially during the search for solutions. Some of the more potent killer phrases are shown in Table 4.2.

Using these rules, a series of *whats* are generated, and for each *what* a series of *hows* will spell out an implementation strategy complete with

it won't work	yes, but
too academic	it's too early
too modern	it's too late
common sense	nuts
haven't the time	political dynamite
too old-fashioned	people won't do it
not in the budget	let's wait and see
we tried that once	the union will scream
we're too small	not our problem
we're too big	not in the manual
no outsider can tell me how to run my business	costs too much
you don't understand the problem	let's form a committee to study it

Table 4.2. Killer phrases used to stop the flow of ideas.

assigned resources and due dates for activity completion. Again, from our composite example, under *staffing* a subset of training was established with the following management recognition statement:

> The analysis and programming training program is not in concert with IS department goals and objectives. (Note that elsewhere it had been established that the IS department had no stated goals and objectives.)

In other words, there was no goal-oriented training program for analysts and programmers. No doubt money was being spent on training, but to what purpose? The following *whats* and *hows* were generated as solutions to the training problem:

> *What*—define organizational responsibilities as they relate to training.

> *How*—define responsibility for training and submit to managers for agreement.

> *What*—determine analyst and programmer training guidelines to meet overall goals and objectives.

> *What*—perform a basic skills assessment of each programmer/ analyst and determine each one's ability to support work load demands.

> *How*—request that training division perform a skills survey and match against work load demands.

> *What*—tailor training courses to work load demands and skills survey results rather than continuing to use off-the-shelf materials.

> *How*—request that training division provide approaches for tailoring courses.

Due dates for assigned activities were established and appropriate written directions were given.

Dealing with Structural Management Problems: How Big an Effort?

What is the level of effort required for a management team to take these initial steps in creating an environment for success? First, a word of caution: The size of the IS department probably has no bearing on the type and number of structural management problems facing the management team. These problems result from the nature of the IS business—its newness, complexity, and uncertainties. Some may think that small organizations have small problems. This is decidedly not true! Small IS groups have the same type of problems as large groups because the same management functions must be performed whether the group numbers 10 or 1000.

Further, the complexity of the technology and the uncertainties of its use do not diminish with organizational size. In fact, the opposite is true. The problems of managing information technology are even more severe because they are concentrated on fewer managers. The fewer the managers, the more important it is to surface and deal with structural management problems in an organized no-nonsense manner.

From consulting experience, the following averaged numbers may be helpful.

Structural management problems	20 to 30
Management categories	6 to 8
Management recognition statements	6 to 8
Solutions—*whats*	50 to 60
Assignments—*hows*	70 to 90

Where can we possibly find the time to carry out 70 to 90 assignments, not to mention time spent coming up with the problem statements and solutions? How can we work it in? We are too busy trying to run this place, too busy putting out fires!"

This is what top management commitment means!

If Deming is right, and the conditions described in this book correct, then IS quality and productivity improvements cannot be made until IS management processes have been put in order! This will require a considerable effort on the part of all IS managers, and especially the CIO!

Remember that the IS department should be able to manage all current or planned activities by showing a positive relationship between the activity and the following questions:

- What will the activity do to improve the quality of IS products or services?

- If the activity is not helping our customers reach their quality goals, why are we doing it?
- If the activity is not helping to reduce our cost of quality, why are we doing it?

Without the focus of these three questions, there is no benchmark against which to measure the quality impact of current information practices and future initiatives. By viewing the IS business through these three questions, IS department management is ready to tackle the technical journey required of TQM.

5 TQM and Management of the SDP II: Requirements Definition

Introduction

Now that top management's involvement is ensured and an environment for systems development success is being created, the principles of TQM can be applied to the SDP itself.

As discussed earlier, the SDP is a TQM-compatible model used by IS professionals to define, construct, and deliver systems. Let us examine the DRT portion of Figure 4.1 (on page 46) to see how the application of contemporary development concepts, methods, tools, and techniques can be used to implement TQM principles during requirements definitions.

DRT and Requirements Definition

First, there are many contemporary concepts and methods being promoted as instrumental in performing the requirements definition phase of the SDP. A partial list includes the following:

- Enterprise modeling

- Information engineering

- Business reengineering

- Business area analysis

- Business case analysis
- Business process improvement
- Business process redesign

All of these concepts and methods are attempting to *do right things (DRT)* through analysis of the customer's requirement.

These concepts and methods employ various approaches, tools, and techniques to assist in this analysis and to capture the results, such as the following:

- Structured analysis
- Data modeling
- Process modeling
- Computer-assisted systems engineering (CASE)
- Joint application development
- Object-oriented approaches

These methods and techniques are vast improvements over the requirements analysis methods of the past. All allow a more sophisticated use of today's technologies. Each represents an implementation of *structured* thinking in an attempt to impose an engineering discipline on the process of the SDP. Each also promotes and implements the following TQM principles:

- Meeting requirements through customer focus
- Error-free work through preventive thinking
- Use of problem-solving techniques

Note that the use of these analysis techniques and tools is aimed at getting closer to the true business requirement of the customer. The business requirements as represented by Figure 1.3 (on page 6).

Requirements Definition Concurrent with TQM Work Process Analysis

As previously discussed, a major reason for customer dissatisfaction with the work-products of the IS department seems to lie in the failure to address workplace and organizational aspects in the technical system design. Put another way, if the workplace and organizational impact of an information system is not taken into account, the effort is likely to fail or be marginally successful even if technical systems quality is not in question.

Do contemporary concepts, tools, and technologies of the SDP address these social and organizational issues? Generally speaking, no! But only because they are not being used in the environment where such issues are being addressed. They are not being used during a customer's TQM improvement analysis of a work process. These concepts, methods, and techniques should be used to record the information and process requirements that are identified during a customer's TQM deliberations. This provides an important first step in achieving the overall goal of business redesign. An excellent source document to assist in this analysis is *Information Technology and Organizational Change*.[13]

Figure 5.1 depicts the complementary relationship that exists between two currently popular analytic approaches and the TQM workprocess examination. The figure illustrates that both information engineering and business process redesign can benefit from a concurrent TQM workprocess examination. Likewise, a TQM workprocess examination is more complete and representative of the total business requirement when supported by the thinking of both information engineering and business process analysis.

All three of these analytic approaches, in combination, create a much more complete picture of the customer's requirement than does any one method alone. The recent evolution of information system requirements analysis techniques has also progressed to the point where detailed business process and information needs can be captured and specified through the use of automated tools. Missing, however, is the perspective brought by a TQM workprocess analysis, namely the actual workplace aspects represented by the right-hand side of Figure 1.3. Not until all of the sociotechnical and business requirements are addressed will customer-oriented improvements be realized in the development and delivery of information systems. Not until customer-oriented requirements are met will the quality of systems, as perceived by the customer, improve appreciably!

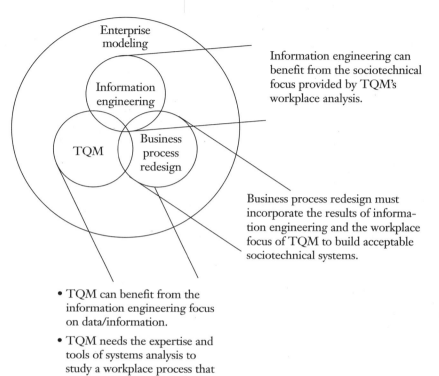

Figure 5.1. Complementary relationships.

In fact, business area analysis, business redesign, or business reengineering efforts can only be marginally successful unless they are accomplished *concurrent* with a TQM workprocess analysis. Without this combined perspective, failure to meet the sociotechnical requirements of Figure 1.3 will continue.

In addition to addressing the social and workplace aspects in a design, what else would be accomplished by the concurrent performance of an information requirements and TQM workprocess analysis? Since virtually all information requirements and specifications find their origins in knowledge of the business process, it is during the analysis of the business process that the quality attributes of the information and processing system should be addressed. Note also that these same quality attributes must form the customer's final acceptance criteria for the finished system!

Expanding the customary definition of *user* to reflect the *customer-provider* paradigm will open up the requirement definition phase of the SDP considerably. If our goal is to apply the DRT concept to the requirements definition, then we must be very circumspect in regards to who participates in this phase.

First, the community of customers must be thoroughly researched, and those with any stake or interest in the system must participate in requirements definition. A representative sample of interested customers or stakeholders for most systems would include

- Customers performing the business function (internal)
- Customers of the enterprise (external)
- Customer management (internal)
- Contract officials
- Internal and external auditors
- Security administrators
- Operations managers
- Software maintenance personnel
- Executive management
- Shareholders and oversight groups
- The legal department

This list speaks to the ever-expanding influence of information systems in business, government, and society.

The identification of customers is sometimes difficult for there are extended end-use customers for many systems. For example, who are the end-use customers of many governmental information systems? The answer is the American public and American business. In these instances of course, not every customer can be involved in a requirements analysis, so their representatives (for example, government agency officials) must be especially conscious to present the public interest. Nowhere is this called for more than in the case of maintaining accurate information on citizens and protecting confidentiality. This quality-of-information issue has been deemed important enough for Congress to pass various pieces of legislation, most notably the Privacy Act of 1974. The Privacy Act views the quality-of-information issue to be so important that civil sanctions are allowed against the federal government if the government uses inaccurate information about a citizen, thus causing harm to the person.

Second, there must be agreement with customers on the definition of quality that will be used to guide the development effort. As seen in chapter 2, there are five definitions of quality, each with a decidedly different impact on the SDP. Only one definition is reasonable for most system development projects, and that is the *manufacturing-based* definition of conformance to requirements.

Identification of Quality Attributes and Metrics

From the representative sample of customers will come differing requirements for quality. Customers will perceive the quality of the information system in light of their own business needs. The list of quality attributes is long and varied, but will generally include the following:

accuracy	auditable
timeliness	documentable
reliability	maintainable
testability	survivable
security	accessible
consistency	usable

Beyond each of these are the attributes that senior management desire in order to obtain efficient business activity and to optimize the technological investment:

effective

adaptable

expandable

efficient

portable

reusable

interoperable

At best, trying to satisfy all customers and all interests is an extremely difficult juggling act. All customers will have their business requirements to satisfy, and some of these requirements may conflict with those of other, equally important, customers. Some requirements, by their very nature, will conflict with others. Accessibility will always conflict with security, while efficiency conflicts with such attributes as usability, maintainability, and portability. For example, each of these requires additional coding, processing, or some other form of overhead to give transparency and flexibility. These stand to conflict with the efficiencies of optimizing code. But today, except in rare cases, optimizing code is a throwback to the days when memory was expensive and processing slow. In most cases optimizing code at the expense of customer-oriented or ease-of-maintenance attributes is a poor choice indeed. It continues to ignore the needs of customers and perpetuates unnecessary complexity in systems and software. It provides a false economy.

In a practical sense the definition of quality attributes, as perceived by each customer and the trade-off of conflicting requirements, cannot be made by IS personnel. In the past system analysts have often been forced to make such decisions and, in each case, have paid a heavy price. Such quality definitions and trade-off decisions can only be made in light of the business process requirements and only by the managers of the business process.

A concurrent performance of information requirements definition and TQM workprocess analysis can correct this serious impediment to the goal of DRT. Concurrent analysis will ensure customer focus and will result in comprehensive requirements that reflect

- The functional business requirement
- The social aspects of the system
- The workplace processing requirements
- The complete quality attribute and trade-off analysis
- Top management commitment since trade-off decisions affecting the business process will have to be made

From these requirements and decisions will come the automated IS requirements and a clear understanding of the quality attribute metrics against which the final systems product will be judged. Through concurrent analysis, the Figure 1.2 (on page 4) dilemma of identifying the proper division of labor between humans and computers can also be resolved.

With more complete knowledge of the business problem, the social workplace requirement, and the customer quality requirements to be satisfied, the IS department can finally design and develop information systems that stand a chance of meeting customer expectations, thereby raising the success rate of system acceptance.

This is not to imply, however, that all customer requirements will be satisfied through the efforts of the IS analyst. They cannot! Certainly, the majority of the topics constituting the right-hand section of Figure 1.3 (on page 6) are not within the province of the IS department to change. There is always the need for a parallel design and development effort to be going on in the workplace to address these topical areas. Work flow, training, job design, and personnel policies must be modified. This degree of modification can be determined during the concurrent execution of the information requirements and TQM workprocess analysis. This critical task, which systematically changes both the automated system and the accompanying workplace and social system, is at the heart of *business process redesign!*

Preventive Thinking During the Requirements Phase

Meeting and managing customer expectations is the *key factor* to reaching the goal of DRTRFT. In order to meet those expectations, what else does TQM suggest we do during the early phases of the SDP? What else must occur, in addition to obtaining a clear, concise understanding of quality attributes? What will aid in managing customer expectations for the system?

TQM suggests that we practice *preventive thinking!* Preventive thinking that results in risk aversion should take place during the requirements definition. The *what if* analysis of preventive thinking needs to focus on potential problems that could adversely affect information quality or process integrity.

Preventive thinking asks that the system developers of both the automated portion of the system and the *workplace* portion of the system identify threats to information quality and process or systems integrity. What conditions exist that could compromise the quality of information or render the process and system unreliable?

This is where the expertise and experience of some of our participating customers should be utilized. This is the realm of security studies, risk analysis, and the identification of audit and internal controls to prevent or detect fraud and system abuse.

Stakeholders from these expert areas have great knowledge of how systems have been compromised or unlawfully exploited in the past. Much has been written over the last 20 years on these subjects. Now is the time to address the building of secured and trusted systems by having these experts participate in preventive thinking and in proposing corrective actions for problems that are identified.

Methodologies, such as those presented by Richard Baskerville in *Designing Information Systems Security*[14] should be applied at this point of the SDP. Numerous other books, federal government guidelines, and National Institute of Standards and Technology (NIST) and international standards should be applied at this stage of the SDP.

Preventive thinking allows us to protect the extra effort that has been expended during the requirements definition to obtain clear and concise quality definitions. Without preventive thinking, even though we may have accomplished much to attain our goal of DRT, we risk failure during the system construction phase of the SDP because we will not be aware of potential threats to information quality and process integrity. If we can anticipate these vulnerabilities, we can define and design preventive, detective, and recovery measures. Or, at the very least, we can present these vulnerabilities to customer management, illicit the desired course of action, and in the process better manage the customer's expectations for the final system.

To the benefit of the IS department, participation by stakeholder experts (that is, security, auditors, and so on) takes a great deal of heat off the developers since quality trade-off decisions never please anyone totally, and it is the enterprise's management, not IS analysts, that must now make those decisions.

Validation Ensures DRT

Referring back to Figure 4.1 (on page 46), three quality assurance activities are identified for the purpose of ensuring that the goals of DRT and RFT are actually attained. These activities are validation, verification, and test.

Before the TQM mantra of DRTRFT, there was validation (that is, *Are we doing the right thing?*), and verification (that is, *Are we doing it right?*). Both of these quality assurance activities use various review and confirmation techniques to ensure DRT and RFT. The activity of validation is especially critical during the requirement definition phase of the SDP. Before large commitments of time, money, and personnel are expended in construction, it is wise to affirm that we are going to construct what the customer needs—that we have defined and agreed upon all requirements.

There are well-documented techniques for performing these tasks. In fact, there are international organizations that exist for the sole purpose of promoting use of these techniques during systems development (for example, ASQC and the Quality Assurance Institute). These quality assurance tasks can be performed internally by the systems development team, or, as is becoming more common, the validation function can be performed by an independent group to guarantee objectivity.

The power of contemporary SDP tools and techniques make this task easier to perform now than in the past. The use of structured methodologies supported by CASE tools makes the validation review activity accessible to all participating customers and stakeholders, and tracks all validated requirements for accountability during the remainder of the SDP.

The performance of validation activities during the concurrent execution of the information requirements and the TQM workprocess analysis will have a profound effect in attainment of the future line of Figure 2.2 (on page 24).

Validation, as a quality assurance activity, confirms customer requirements and uncovers errors, omissions, or misunderstandings that, if allowed to stand, will cost considerably more to correct during a later phase of the development effort.

Conclusion

This chapter has attempted to make the following points:

1. The concept of DRT is fully compatible with IS thinking and workprocesses as embodied in the traditional SDP.

2. Most of the analysis tools and techniques used by TQM in problem solving are already in the tool kit of the IS department. This allows both the IS customer and the IS analyst to work together to define a complete set of sociotechnical requirements for the business support system.

3. The fact that many customers on the functional side of the business are employing TQM problem-solving techniques works to the advantage of the IS department and provides a common language (quality) around which to pursue comprehensive business redesign efforts using contemporary methodologies, tools, and techniques.

4. An emphasis on front-end analysis combining information requirements and the TQM work-process analysis buys the enterprise the following:

   • An increased probability of delivering quality information through reliable processes

   • Better, more complete project planning to reduce late SDP waste and rework

   • Management of customer expectations through involvement in both the requirements definition and in the validation of those requirements

   • Higher confidence in the stability of the requirements and the quality metrics to be used to judge final systems delivery

   • A better understanding of project and functional application risk through preventive thinking

   • A reduction of the likelihood of cost overruns since knowledge of the system to be constructed is so much better

   • Improved communications with the customers of the information system

Finally, through the quality assurance activity of validation, we practice the carpenter's axiom of *measure twice, cut once.*

6   TQM and Management of the SDP III: Construction and Delivery

Introduction

The right-hand side of Figure 4.1 (on page 46) is the topic of discussion for this chapter.

Having just expended extra effort and resources to obtain clear, concise, and measurable information and processing requirements, it would be a shame if IS execution of the latter phases of the SDP resulted in doing it wrong.

Thus far we have presented an application of TQM philosophies and principles to the business of IS when dealing with customer requirements and when addressing the internal management of the IS department. We have

- Established the need to improve our focus on customer requirements and have seen how contemporary systems analysis methods, tools, and techniques can assist with this

- Applied the goal of DRTRFT to the SDP, the core business process of the IS department

- Started the continuous improvement journey beginning at the top of the IS management structure by addressing any behavioral and management problems that may inhibit attempts to DRTRFT

- Applied preventive thinking to the identification of quality attribute measures, performance criteria, and system maintenance issues, and to the definition of system security and reliability requirements

- Applied preventive thinking to identify project risk indicators and management problems that make RFT impossible

- Established a problem-solving and corrective action process to address project risk indicators and management problems on a continuing basis

- Used this application of TQM to obtain and sustain top management commitment through participation in the necessary trade-off decisions and in providing business justifications that support automation initiatives

It is now time to apply TQM to the technical journey on which the IS department has embarked. In the experience of many IS veterans, this technical journey is what drives the organization, as opposed to meeting customer requirements!

The IS manager is virtually inundated with technical solutions. Most of the time, these are solutions in search of a problem. All too often today's pressing problem turns out to be yesterday's solution now in the throes of implementation. Magic bullets appear to be everywhere. *Management by magazine* is often the norm. Due to the speed of technological change, the poor quality of products and services from other IS industry sources (that is, other providers of hardware, software, networks, and so on), the lack of adherence to standards, and the fierce competitive nature of the industry, most IS departments spend an inordinate amount of time and energy just getting pieces of the technology to play.

Technological advances in hardware (i.e., where we seem to direct all our attention) have created mammoth opportunities for developers to offer seemingly endless software variations without actually inventing a new software product. One result . . . is that a lot of business software is designed as an adventure game. Here are the rules of the game: you must hit the right buttons at the right time and you win; if you strike the wrong key, you lose. Do not attempt to play without reading the READ ME file or the documentation, which has been shrink-wrapped for your protection, or the assorted inserts that have been included to update the erroneous documentation in the manual.

Somehow along the way, the software development establishment seems to have successfully convinced the buying public and technophiles who write product reviews, that software has a right to be defective. New software always has a few bugs, we are smugly and patronizingly informed.[15]

The net impact of this reality is that our customer is short-changed. Either the IS department is unnecessarily absorbed in getting the technology to play, or the technology, arcane rules and all, is passed onto the customer to deal with.

Most users simply want a no-nonsense product that installs quickly and does the job without blowing up when you hit the wrong key. . . . Users want a system that is "forgiving" when they are in a novice mode and sophisticated when they are ready to stretch. . . . Most users don't really care about a graphical user interface.

Techies and game players love high-resolution, animated color graphics because they understand how elegant and hard it is to accomplish. If you ask them, though, most business professionals would gladly trade cute little icons for a product that was easy to install and safe to use. . . . Yet many users today still can't get the information they need without learning how to write code. . . . There are too many technical complexities for most business people to deal with. The user should not have to adjust the way he does a job to the quirks of the machine, software, keyboard or mouse.[16]

Construction and delivery of quality information products and services in a technological environment of such virtual chaos surely stretches the capabilities of most IS departments. Can TQM help get such chaos under control? Can TQM philosophies and principles assist in stabilizing and improving the construction and delivery activities of the SDP? Can the IS department ever hope to accomplish RFT?

Identify and Measure Cost of Quality

Cost of quality is the sum of all those costs experienced by the IS department in providing the customer with a quality information product or service. By identifying and measuring the cost of quality, we establish a baseline understanding of current quality-related expenditures against which future improvements and savings can be compared. These are the positive costs of problem prevention and inspection and the negative costs of waste, rework, and scrap.

Referring back to chapter 2, we are reminded that we need to identify the negative costs of waste, scrap, and rework, associated with the shaded area of Figure 2.2 (on page 24).

Such costs result when

- Right things are done wrong.
- Wrong things are done right.
- Wrong things are done wrong.

To identify these costs, the IS department's internal accounting systems need to be able to differentiate, on a task-by-task basis, between original effort expended on meeting a requirement and the rework necessary to finally satisfy the customer. There is also the need to identify hard computing resources expended in support of rework.

Next, there are certain customer-related costs that need to be factored into an overall cost of quality. These are the costs experienced by customers as they attempt to perform their work in spite of poor quality information products and services, such as the following:

- Faulty decisions based on faulty information
- Inaccurate reports on resource usage and project status
- Customer costs associated with working *around* the system

- Customer rework due to hardware and software problems
- Missed scheduled deliveries
- Late or inaccurate shipments
- Overpayments and underpayments
- Missed discounts
- Loss of credibility with external customers and potential liabilities

This identification of the customer's cost of quality demonstrates once again the linchpin phenomenon and vividly illustrates why attempted TQM improvements to business processes must include the IS department, and must be accomplished jointly.

Once this link is established and the size of the actual combined waste and rework is identified, the motivation for improving internal IS department construction and delivery processes will be overwhelming. This accumulation of negative costs can be used in an overall strategy to justify the positive costs of better and more comprehensive analysis and planning. Negative costs can also be used to justify improvements to the IS department infrastructure and for training.

Establishing SDP Measures as a Baseline for Performance Improvement

The TQM focus on process with the goal of achieving continuous improvement means we must establish baseline information about our quality performance. We must know what kind of problems are occurring and what rework really costs. From an enterprise perspective, how well does our IS department measure up against other IS organizations? Are we competitive? Are we getting our dollar's worth? Before improvements can be made, a baseline or snapshot of where we are must be developed. Only then can progress be charted and credibility of IS work products be restored.

Reviewing, for a moment, the conditions found to contribute to high-risk development efforts (Table 4.1 on page 46), it will be seen that many of those listed find their origin in the lack or inaccuracy of historical resource measurement and utilization data. Inadequate planning and budgeting, unrealistic cost and time estimates, and abandonment of plans are directly related to a lack of historic measurement data concerning previous projects. Without such data, it is virtually impossible for a development effort to start off on the right foot!

Due to the inability to generate meaningful project plans, budgets, and realistic estimates and scheduling, the entire execution of the SDP is compromised from the very beginning. The first casualty is the time required to adequately define requirements. Without being able to determine, through analysis, all of the requirements, plus quality and performance metrics, complexity and uncertainty cannot be factored in. Project resource and time estimates become guesses, pure and simple. Baseless estimates and delivery promises are rendered and customer expectations become unsupportable!

The net result is that the construction and delivery phases of the SDP become driven by customer expectations of a political nature that are not tempered by a calculated attempt to DRTRFT. This means that the RFT practices for systems construction and delivery, which include disciplined analysis, design, and software engineering, will be under intense pressure to speed up, compress, shorten, consolidate, or entirely eliminate certain functions. Typically, this means that requirements are not validated, designs do not receive proper reviews, comprehensive testing is disallowed, documentation is never complete, and training is catch-as-catch-can. Then everyone wonders why the development was unsuccessful.

TQM applied to the SDP requires that measurement become integral to managing, so that future project estimates will be realistic and defensible. Two recommended readings before setting up a measurement activity include *Applications Strategies for Risk Analysis*,[17] and *Software Engineering Economics*.[18]

The next aspect of measurement deals with the identification of types and sources of errors and their occurrences. For example, does an incidence of rework or other corrective action find its origin in faulty, changing, or misunderstood requirements, a poor design, or improper construction and delivery of the final system? Information identifying where rework occurs, time spent on rework, and causes for rework must be gathered and analyzed. With TQM discussions of measurement, the principle technique offered is the reliance on statistical process control, which sets strict, quantitative levels against which the product under development is measured. When products do not meet these criteria, the development process is changed to achieve the necessary improvement.

With regard to information systems development, the primary criteria against which the product is measured is the customer's information and systems requirement with all quality and performance attributes satisfied. In the systems business customers seldom have the exact same information requirement; and while hardware may be statistically stable, the actual meeting of the customer's information need is accomplished through software—thought by many to be more an art than a science.

A secondary criteria deals with the efficiency with which systems are constructed (that is, programmed). Since software is more art than science, statistical process control has not been easy to adopt and may not be totally applicable.

Today, if the system products under development are not meeting customer requirements, then we look to change the process whereby the requirement is defined and the process whereby the system is constructed, validated, verified, and tested. While the application of strict statistical process control is premature for most IS departments, the underlying concept of conformance to requirements applies. Measurement activities will eventually build the databases required for more precise statistical control of future construction activities.

The last area of consideration under measurement deals with the human element. Having established error-free work as the goal of the organization, are personnel properly educated and trained to accomplish the goal? Figure 6.1 depicts areas of consideration requiring constant attention and monitoring if the IS department is to deliver quality products and move in the desired technical direction while meeting the needs of the customer. The first three areas to consider are

- Market and customer need
- Project and delivery management
- Technical direction

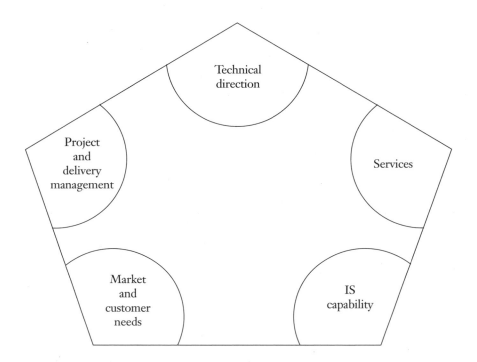

Figure 6.1. Customer focus issues.

Once these areas have been analyzed to determine the appropriateness and quality of services being offered, the IS department must then examine its capability to deliver those services.

A capability to deliver requires the proper mix of computing resources and competent personnel. The measurement challenge is to determine these core competencies and map them against the requirement to define, build, and deliver the error-free services set as the goal for the organization.

Using this information, IS management will be much better equipped to forecast future training requirements, to formulate individual development plans for employees, and to devise realistic career paths within the organization. It is generally conceded that growing your own is desirable if there appears to be a long-term need. This deliberate attempt to define core competencies and create realistic training programs improves employee morale, reduces turnover, and makes for efficient use of training dollars. It also provides a rationale for the training budget in the first place.

Refine Cost of Quality Using Measurement Data

Concentrating our focus on continuous improvement requires reinforcement that the effort is worthwhile. Updating and refining the cost of quality, as process improvements begin to bear tangible results, will provide such reinforcement. The initial cost of quality estimates will be rough and will be represented by IS department cost and customer cost. It is critical to refine not only the system cost figures but the customer's cost figures as well. This action will assist in nurturing the partnership and customer focus mentality so important to TQM.

Evaluating the SDP: Establishing a Baseline for Continuous Improvement

This aspect of TQM implementation gets to the heart of the IS business process used to define, construct, and deliver information systems—the SDP. There are three major areas to be addressed in evaluating the SDP and in formulating a continuous improvement strategy.

- The IS department's level of sophistication in executing the SDP

- The identification of specific SDP improvements using cost of quality and measurement data to pinpoint areas for improvement

- The evaluation of alternative SDP models for use on projects, based on the characteristics of the development effort and the system to be constructed

Sophistication in using a systems development process should be measured using the evaluation techniques developed by the Software Engineering Institute (SEI) at Carnegie-Mellon University. The Institute was established in 1984 to address the well-recognized need for improving software and systems in the U.S. Department of Defense. An important initial step in addressing software problems is to treat the entire development task as a process that can be controlled, measured, and improved. The philosophy, approach, and techniques of the Institute provide a tried and tested methodology for making quality improvements to the software development aspect of the SDP.

To improve their software capabilities, organizations need to take five basic steps:[19]

1. Understand the current status of their development process.

2. Develop a vision of the desired process.

3. Establish a list of required process improvement actions in order of priority.

4. Produce a plan to accomplish these actions.

5. Commit the resources to execute the plan.

While this is clearly a traditional approach, note that the TQM principles of *measurement, preventive thinking*, and *problem-solving/corrective actions* are imbedded in the five steps. Note also that the *cost of quality* principle provides the motivational impetus to initiate and continue through the five steps until quality and cost improvements are made.

The SEI provides a framework for characterizing the SDP at a series of maturity levels. Figure 6.2 depicts the five levels.

The levels are defined by the SEI in the following way:[20]

1. Initial—could properly be called ad hoc or chaotic. Here the IS department operates without formalized plans. Even if formal procedures are developed, there is no management mechanism to ensure that they are used. The best test is to observe how such an organization behaves in a crisis. If it abandons established procedures and reverts to merely coding and unit testing, it is likely to be at the initial level.

2. Repeatable—this level of maturity has one important strength over the initial level. It provides a reasonable measure of management commitment to control. The IS department at this level has instituted certain SDP controls. Among these are

   • Project management

The goal:

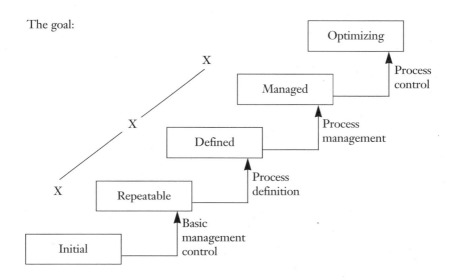

Figure 6.2. SDP maturity levels.

- Management oversight
- Product assurance
- Change control

This level represents a growing degree of competence at doing the same type of systems work over and over again—repeatable. New technology and new challenges, however, can present a new mix of risks that the SDP is not equipped to handle.

  3. Defined process—at this level, the IS department has taken steps for making major and continuing progress. These steps include:

   - Establishment of a process group to focus on improving execution and management of the SDP. This may include a structural decomposition of tasks, improvements to those tasks, and implementation assignments.

   - If not already in place, introduction of a family of software engineering methods, technologies, and tools is now in order.

4. Managed process—advancement to the managed level incorporates the TQM principles of measurement and cost of quality into the structured long-term strategy for systems and software development by:

   • Establishing a basic set of process measures to identify quality and cost parameters at each step of the SDP

   • Building a measurements database and manage it

   • Analyzing the data to identify SDP areas that need improvement

5. Optimized process—the step to final maturity occurs when the measurement data and cost parameter data gathered at level four are used to actually fine-tune the SDP itself rather than to focus on the product. At this level of maturity, the IS department has the means to identify the weakest elements of the SDP and take action to correct them. The two fundamental requirements are

   • Providing automated tool support for gathering process data, thus

   • Turning management's focus to process and from product.

Implementation of the SEI Maturity Model begins with an assessment covering three areas of systems and software development.

1. Organization and resource management

2. The software engineering process of the IS group and its management

3. Tools and technology

In all, there are over 100 questions assessing the SDP and another 10 or so assessing the experience level of personnel involved in software engineering.

Although not well known outside of the Department of Defense, the SEI Evaluation Program provides a ready-made approach for initiating a continuous improvement effort for the SDP.

For IS departments that are not primarily into systems or software development, the essence of the SEI approach can be tailored for specific use. While some of the questions in the evaluation would be different, the criteria, rationale, and framework of level advancement from ad hoc to structured management would still apply and could be used to map future improvements. Caution, however, is called for: The SEI approach is not a substitute for an internal TQM initiative! It is a readily available evaluation technique for assessing a portion of the technical infrastructure. It has nothing to do with the cultural/behavioral journey, and it does not provide any vehicle for identifying or dealing with the *structural management problems* we have seen that can make DRTRFT impossible.

Continuous improvement of the SDP is based on measurement and cost of quality. Over the long haul areas for quality and productivity improvement are to be identified by using cost of quality and the measurement system to highlight areas for attention. Combined with the SEI maturity model, an IS department will be able to map out and plan a logical, defensible strategy for using available tools, techniques, and practices to further its quality improvement goals. This same rationale can also be used to determine new technologies for use and control their introduction into the workplace.

In cooperation with the customer, justification for new tools and methods will be eased because customers will be able to articulate how such improvements to the IS infrastructure will benefit themselves. This, of course, means that cost of quality and measurement monitoring become continuous activities of the IS department management team. These are basic to the management of any function and, therefore, cannot be considered too onerous. In fact, the necessity for these activities has already been identified as solutions to some of the structural management problems identified by IS department managers as reasons why they cannot DRTRFT.

Cost of quality, measurement, and continuous improvement at every level forms the basis for kaizen. Figure 6.3 depicts kaizen as

> a Japanese term used to describe improvements that, over time, leapfrog the competitors who are depending on technological breakthroughs alone. Workers, supported by managers, are the major source of these improvements. Applying kaizen to routine work is the key to success.[21]

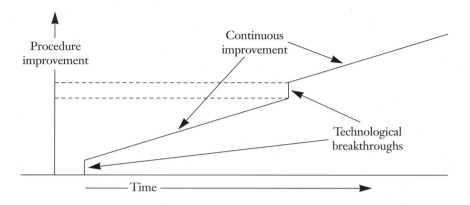

Figure 6.3. Continuous improvement by means of kaizen.

Kaizen has become a model for the dramatic improvements that CEOs and stockholders dream about, but it requires the disciplined continuous application, day by day, of all TQM principles and philosophies to become a reality.

Choosing among alternative SDP models is a decision driven by many risk factors associated with the complexity and uncertainty of the system under development and the risks posed by the structural management problems previously identified.

Considerations affecting the choice of the SDP model, from among those available, could read like a summary of this document. First, the target goal of the SDP model must be to provide quality information to the customer by constructing processing systems that have integrity and can be trusted. Second, the choice of the SDP model should empower the IS department to DRTRFT, thus improving the cost of quality curve. Third, the choice of the SDP model should improve productivity, but only as a by-product of quality improvement. Fourth, the chosen SDP model should be comprehensive in scope and foster good management practices as well as *sound* system development practices.

There are a number of SDP models often referred to as life-cycle methodologies. Summarized, there are four general models to consider:[22]

- Waterfall/design-driven (used throughout this document for illustrative purposes)

- Rapid-prototype/interactive
- Operational/process-driven
- Spiral/risk-driven

Each model has some measure of advantage and risk associated with it. The waterfall/design driven model represents a model that is intuitively attractive, and has an experienced user base behind it. The rapid-prototype model . . . develops the system incrementally, and provides rapid feedback to the developers and users. The operational model produces specifications that are executable . . . and tightens the link between what is specified and what is implemented. The spiral model uses risk as its main parameter to drive the model forward. . . . Each of the process models described have some deficiency that makes it difficult to use as is. . . . The waterfall/design driven model is very restrictive in its monolithic approach. . . . It fails to specifically include activities . . . such as project or configuration management, does not provide for feedback . . . concerning the quality of the system being built. . . . The rapid-prototype model overcomes most of these deficiencies, but includes some of its own. . . . The primary deficiencies are that . . . incremental development makes management coordination difficult. This is exacerbated because there is no clear separation between iterations. Further, like the waterfall model, it wasn't designed specifically for automation. On the other hand, the operational . . . models are specifically geared for automation, but focus primarily on the process of developing a software system. The management aspect is implicit, rather than explicit, just like the waterfall model. The spiral model requires a thorough understanding of risk engineering to work effectively.

Clearly, the choice of SDP model must be carefully determined, perhaps with an eye to different models being used under different circumstances. Whatever the technical issues involved, it is imperative that the choice of SDP model be heavily weighed by the quality assurance functions and management controls imposed on the use of the model.

In addition to selecting an SDP model that improves our ability to DRT during requirements definitions, it must also facilitate RFT during construction and delivery by requiring

- Comprehensive project management
- Configuration management
- Validation, verification, and testing
- Adherence to structured techniques
- Technology transfer plans
- Complete usable documentation
- Measurement recording

Of course, the chosen model should be consistent with the actions the IS department management team identified as solving its structural management problems. Final customer satisfaction must be the goal of all IS development and the appropriate SDP model will, if managed, facilitate attainment of that goal.

Validation, Verification, and Testing Ensures RFT

DRTRFT has a price. That price, so far, has been the preventive cost of quality associated with getting the customer's requirement right during the requirements definition phase of the SDP (Figure 4.1 on page 46). There has also been a cost of quality associated with correcting our structural management problems and creating the environment for success. It would be a real shame to drop the quality ball now!

The quality assurance activities of validation, verification, and test ensure that our quality investments to this point are not being undermined through faulty construction of the system.

In an earlier discussion validation (are we doing the right thing) techniques were used to obtain agreement with the customer as to what we were going to build and deliver. Now we must execute the construction phase of the SDP and ensure that, even with our clear, concise, and customer-validated requirement, we do not introduce design errors and commit programming and/or integration errors that result in a non-quality product or service.

Figure 6.4 illustrates the avalanche-of-errors phenomenon that overwhelms most development efforts. Verification activities provide evidence that the process of systems construction is meeting requirements and using sound design and programming practices. According to ANSI/IEEE Std 729-1983, there are three definitions for verification:[23]

1. The process of determining whether or not the products of a given phase of the SDP fulfill the requirements established during a previous phase

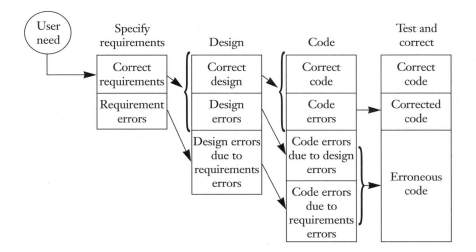

Figure 6.4. Avalanche of errors.

2. Formal proof of program corrections

3. The act of reviewing, inspecting, testing, checking, auditing, or otherwise establishing and documenting whether or not items, processes, services, or documents conform to specified requirements

Historically, verification has been limited to testing, and testing was limited to the testing of code at module, subsystem, or system level. Such testing culminated in user acceptance testing, a form of validation accomplished to evaluate whether the final delivered system complied with original requirements. Over the years it has been realized that verification should take place on all items produced during development. For example, you should verify the

- System specifications (that is, all functional, quality attribute, and performance specifications)
- System design
- Database
- Quality of the programming code
- Documentation

Further, verification provides evidence that sound construction techniques are being used during development of the system. It also provides a form for the traceability of requirements, accounting for each throughout the time needed for system construction.

Testing evaluates the various products of the SDP for defects in designs, programs, and/or documentation. Having said that, it must be noted that few IS professionals are trained in any form of testing, and testing is usually treated as an afterthought. According to Crandall,[24]

> For example, after programmers are trained in COBOL, their instructors tell them that when they finish coding, they must test their programs, but they don't tell them how to do it.
>
> It is amazing that in this period of pervasive software development, there are a great many organizations . . .

> indeed, some very well-known companies that do not
> do testing at all! In the university environment, there
> are fewer than 10 software testing courses in the U.S. . . .
> and most of these are theoretical.

There are many books about testing. The one on my shelf has over 600 pages. Certainly testing, like all the other techniques for building quality systems, is not new and is at least understood by a few.

Our familiar insider who snickered about the SDP will break into guffaws concerning the topic of adequate testing. After all, testing is the most ignored activity, second only to documentation, of the SDP. But the importance of testing to the delivery of quality information products and services cannot be argued, and our application of TQM to the SDP will hopefully lessen the tendency to compromise its effectiveness. The actions taken to DRT during the requirement definition phase must now be followed by testing to guarantee RFT during construction.

Our completed specifications (that is, business function, operational, and quality attribute metrics) form the foundation for testing activities. Test plans, scenarios, data, and programs take on a realism never before possible. Because of our concurrent TQM workprocess information requirements studies, we have generated not only complete sociotechnical requirements (Figure 1.3 on page 6), but the comprehensive quality and acceptance criteria against which to conduct testing. This is an immense improvement over past development and testing experiences.

Using customer focus as the guide, how should testing proceed? Within the testing community there are recognized technical "bug" categories. According to Boris Beizer, "What would you do if a programmer told you that the reason you lost a week's work is that there was a type error or an indirect index error?"[25] The customer will probably not understand or care, and the programmer will get no sense of the adverse impact suffered by the customer and the enterprise by such terms. Technical terms are meaningless to the customer and, from a cost of quality perspective, meaningless to the programmer as well.

A customer focus would categorize such a bug in a more dramatic way using terms that convey impact:

- Data corruption
- Data loss
- Processing errors
- Program control loss (crash)
- Cockpit (user-induced) errors

Notice that each of these terms convey a sense of adverse impact directly affecting our customer. Severity of impact also needs to be viewed from a customer perspective. Beizer's bug severity categories are:[26]

1. Mild—the bug's symptoms are aesthetically offensive: for example, misaligned columns in a report.

2. Moderate—misleading or redundant outputs. Bugs that induce cockpit errors.

3. Annoying—more frequent occurrences of the type in 1 and 2 above. Problems are perceived but there are ways around them. The bug may cause others to complain, such as truncating a name, or sending dunning letters for unpaid bills of $00.00. Call a bug annoying if you have cause to curse it daily.

4. Disturbing—the program refuses to do reasonable and legitimate things which it was designed to do. For example, refusing to print page 34 of a 57 page document.

5. Serious—obvious data loss which can be avoided by backups.

6. Very serious—unknown (at first) data loss or corruption.

7. Extreme—All of the above if they're frequent.

8. Intolerable—subtle, creeping corruption of a large database—especially dangerous for numerical data. For example, gradual erosion of the validity of inventory data. The point at which the damage exceeds the cost of the software, the ancillary cost, and all the rest. The point at which litigation starts.

9. Catastrophic—sufficiently dangerous to destroy the entity that uses the system. Typically, by this time, it is you who's being sued or is on trial.

10. And worse—if you think it can't get worse, consider software that corrupts other software, that corrupts other people's data, or software that kills. And software can kill. (Remember the THERAC 25 therapeutic radiation machine in chapter 1.)

A customer's perspective of software and system bugs brings home the importance of verification and testing! These definitions can also serve to highlight other potential costs of quality (such as, litigation) that the enterprise may be risking because of faulty systems. It serves to justify the added time and resources required to guarantee RFT.

Technology Transfer and the Customer

This last critical area of TQM deals with how the IS department communicates with customers. Communications occur throughout the length of the SDP, and so far the IS department has taken steps to improve these communications through the concurrent TQM work process and information requirements studies conducted during the early phases of development. During construction communications was improved among members of the project team through adherence to the discipline of the SDP model.

Technology transfer (that is, installing the final system successfully in the customer's workplace) and systems documentation are the primary communications issues during the final phase of the SDP.

Technology transfer consists of the many forms of bidirectional communication that take place between the IS department and the customer. While system delivery is the end of the SDP, it is actually the beginning of the systems life cycle for the customer. For the quality-sensitive IS department, it is important that this transfer take place in a smooth manner. The aims of technology transfer are as follows:

- Prove, to the customer's satisfaction, that the system works as designed.

- Install the system and all supporting environmental elements as efficiently as possible.
- Train the system users and maintenance personnel.
- Ensure that all critical support items required for continued customer maintenance are documented and provided.

Documentation, as stated earlier, is the second most ignored work product of the SDP, and yet it is, next to hardware, the most visible to the customer. It has long been recognized that the number one threat to software and system viability is the lack of accurate and current documentation. The perception a majority of customers have of the IS department comes through the documentation they must use. The following relates an all-too-familiar story. Beizer recounts this experience with a bad instruction manual.[27]

> The manual's first instructions were:

>> 'We will start by typing 'The quick brown fox jumped over the lazy dogs.' Don't worry if you make a mistake, with BELCHWORD all your stupid fumble-fingered typing mistakes can be easily fixed. Begin by:

>> Type the letter 'T.' Now type the letter 'h.' . . .

>> Now type the last letter 's,' followed by a period. End this sentence by touching the RETURN key.'

> I suffered through five pages of this pap and decided to skip ahead to the meat. On page 20, I was lost by:

>> Produlators are inconclusive when used in conjunction with semaphores. If you want inverse margination, you must read chapters 12 through 14 before continuing, otherwise you may damage your disc drives.

> A bad manual had been "fixed" by tacking-on a patronizing beginning, but with no thought to consistency and the workings of the adult mind. Such manuals are useful only if you don't need them. . . . Few computer users

have the confidence to assert that the instruction manual is garbage—most will assume that the trouble is with themselves.

Everyone suffers from such documentation: the customer, management, the enterprise, but mostly the IS department! It almost appears as if we were purposely trying to make life difficult for our customer. *It is as if we are daring the customer to use our product.* Let's see you do your job now! Bet you can't figure this out! Are we trying to appear superior, clever, confused, or just uncaring toward the customer? Of course, it sells training—training that uses the same confusing materials. Or is this an ultimate form of job security? If they can't figure it out they can never replace me.

If documentation for our external customer is this poor, imagine the condition of documentation passed among internal IS personnel during a development project. If our desire or ability to communicate with cash-carrying customers is so poor, what must it be like among ourselves?

Documentation between phases of the SDP represents the work products of that phase. The SDP documentation depicts the reality of the work done within a phase. For the next phase to produce a quality work product, quality input from the previous phase is required. Once again, ask our IS insider about the quality of documentation pertaining to systems under development. Undoubtedly, you will hear that such documentation is certainly important, but it is never current and up-to-date. Even bread and butter systems running everyday business applications are seldom documented correctly.

How do you change, correct, or enhance a system if you do not know how it operates? Simple, you spend scarce resources researching what the system does and retrodocumenting the system before you can even analyze the impact of a change, a correction, or an enhancement. This is what 70 percent to 80 percent of programmers are doing! This constitutes an immense cost of quality, all because the IS department did not produce and maintain reliable documentation in the first place.

A TQM customer focus emphasizes that documentation performs the following functions across the entire SDP.

- Establishes the understanding between customer and the IS department as to what is to be built and how it is to function
- Passes information concerning requirements and design from one systems development phase to another and from one team component to the next
- Provides the description of what the customer has accepted at the various review points
- Provides reliable representation of the system at any point of development so that meaningful analyses can be performed before changes are allowed
- Provides traceability of requirements
- Provides an interface for the end user and is the end user's window to the system
- Provides the baseline against which system maintenance is performed
- Becomes the most visible, and easily criticized, part of the development effort

Conclusion

In this chapter, the philosophy and principles of TQM have been applied to the construction and delivery phases of the SDP. We have examined the following principles.

- DRTRFT
- Cost of quality
- SDP measures of performance
- Customer focus
- Managing by prevention

We have seen how these principles can result in quality improvements and how the assurance activities of validation, verification, and test ensure such quality.

These TQM principles are wholly consistent with proper systems development practice. They are given a better than fair chance of implementation because the playing field has been leveled through the efforts of the IS management team to correct any long-standing structural management problems that have, to date, stymied past attempts to build quality IS products for our customers.

In chapter 7, we will discuss implementation of a TQM effort inside the IS department. If one is already underway, suggestions for revitalizing it will be presented.

If the reader is still unsure of whether a TQM effort would be worth the fuss, go directly to chapter 8 for motivation!

7 Creating a Quality-Conscious IS Department

Introduction

> The information services industry, having passed through infancy, is struggling to mature through a process of self-definition and self-actualization. . . . To draw an analogy from developmental psychology, the information services industry is learning, as all adolescents learn, that structure and order, when accepted from within rather than imposed from outside, are liberating rather than restricting.
>
> A general feeling in the industry seems to be that as maturity is achieved, the accurate . . . design, development, and delivery of viable systems within budget and to the user's satisfaction will become the norm rather than the exception.[28]

This description of the IS industry indicates that quality improvements will take place as part of the normal course of evolutionary events. While this may be true, there is call for a more revolutionary course of events. A mutation is needed. External environmental forces usually cause mutations; TQM is such a force.

By adopting TQM philosophies and principles, the IS industry can speed up its maturation process in an organized fashion. In chapters 3 through 6, we explored the application of TQM to the technical business of the IS department—building quality systems. In this chapter we will discuss topics associated with applying TQM to the organizational and human resource side of the department.

Although the behavioral journey began with IS managers tackling their structural management problems, the challenge of *talking the talk and walking the walk* still lies ahead. Organizational and cultural change often does not happen by itself, short of crisis. And crisis just does not allow enough reaction time to turn organizational behavior around. Just as with systems development, preventive thinking is needed. Mechanisms for controlled organizational change must be created within the IS department, as well as mechanisms to improve internal communications.

Management of knowledge workers—people who must think for a living (for example, computer people)—requires an atmosphere of trust and openness. With computer people loyalty and purposeful enterprise affiliations are critical. It is just too easy for disgruntlement or apathy to manifest itself in nonquality work. It is too easy for computer people to let their natural *lone-ranger* tendencies run counter to the good of the enterprise. It is too easy to withhold that *one* essential element of information that makes a system work or allows a system to be understood by someone else.

It is also easy for the entrenched bureaucracy of an IS department to make the new employee (trained in disciplined systems development) feel foolish by sending the message and making it known, *We don't do it that way here* (that is, forget what you learned in school if you want to succeed with us).

This can happen with any attempt to change an organization or to introduce new management techniques. It can be very insidious and always successful unless top management is aware of it and takes action to stop it. For example, the way an uncooperative bureaucracy responds to new ideas or change is often as follows:[29]

1. "Lay low"— if you do not want it to succeed then the more you keep out of the way and do not give help and encouragement, the more likelihood there is of failure.

2. "Rely on inertia"—any change process is up against organizational inertia and if you can be too busy when asked the implementation process may come to a halt.

3. "Keep the project complex, hard to coordinate and vaguely defined"—if the goals are ambiguous or too ambitious there is every chance of failure as energy is dissipated in many different directions.

4. "Minimize the implementers' legitimacy and influence"—if the designers are kept as outsiders, other users will probably not allow them to work effectively.

5. "Exploit their lack of inside knowledge"—the change agent probably know very little about the detailed nature of the work and if they are denied this knowledge, the system will probably prove to be inadequate when it is implemented.

Unless such behavior is clearly prohibited by top management, all attempts to implement any change to the status quo will fail.

Walking the walk does not allow the uncooperative elements of bureaucracy to win, to stifle new ideas, to close down open communications, to destroy trust, and to prevent the IS department from maturing.

Turnover and the Cost of Quality

"One key statistic is sufficient to develop a rather depressing picture of the current state of computer people management. The current turnover rate is 35 percent, and . . . has been stable at this figure for the past few years."[30] While some have attributed this to so-called spiraling wage growth, surveys indicate other significant causes. A recent study by the Butler Cox Foundation found that poor management practice was the major cause of turnover within the computing profession.[31]

> Unpublished surveys conducted in a number of major
> Australian organizations have supported the . . . statistics

with poor management communication, unrealistic deadlines, and lack of support by managers for their people being the major causes of dissatisfaction, low morale and resultant turnover. These findings are further supported by articles such as Jeanne Follman's "The Decline of the American Programmer" and Ed Yourdon's "Fear and Loathing in the Land of Programmers."

What does cost of quality make of a 35 percent turnover rate? A 1981 survey by M. Cherlin indicated that the costs to replace an experienced computer person could exceed $20,000.[32] The Butler Cox study put the replacement cost of an experienced professional at $100,000. Statistics show that the average lost time on a project, caused by a team member's resignation, is six weeks. According to the Butler Cox study, in an organization of 100 people, the lost productivity caused by a 35 percent turnover would be over 300 person-weeks or 10 percent of total available work time. This does not account for the cost of missed scheduled deadlines, a reduction in requirements satisfied, and a general decrease in quality due to a six-week slippage with the inevitable shortcuts taken in final SDP phases.

The common management practice of assuming that high turnover is inevitable and beyond the manager's ability to influence is unacceptable and very expensive. If any reality of the IS department should be reduced to cost of quality terms, it would be the turnover reality.

Within the larger context of TQM, cost of quality is used to identify problem areas needing management attention. The general morale and sense of well-being of computer people is certainly an area that requires management attention!

In a time of reduced budgets and increasing pressure to improve productivity, dealing with turnover and other inhibitors to full employee effectiveness must be high on the TQM priority list. It should be obvious that just throwing more technology at these kinds of problems does little except to provide short-term amusement, new care and feeding problems, and renewed pressure by senior enterprise management to increase productivity and show a return on investment.

On the other hand, attention to employee turnover can result in real productivity improvements. Reductions in turnover benefit the IS department and the customer immediately. Recruitment costs are lowered. All types of training costs are reduced, and more benefit is realized from the training that people do get. Quality is improved because project continuity stabilizes. Customer relations also improves because interfacing with IS personnel does not require constant reestablishment.

On the whole, this one area of cost of quality could show impressive results if the proper attention were given to the working environment and the employee relations aspect of the IS department.

Implementing Cultural Change in the IS Department

Structurally, TQM has provided mechanisms to address issues such as poor quality, low productivity, cost overruns, late delivery, low morale, and high staff turnover. The cultural change committees (from chapter 2) are empowered by top management to implement the philosophies and principles of TQM by addressing four major areas that determine the success or failure of the IS department.

- Management
- Measurement
- Education
- Employee involvement

Through these committees the cultural aspects of the IS department are examined and changes devised and implemented that will create an environment promoting quality improvement, employee contribution, and employee self-actualization.

Chapter 3 described how IS department management takes the first critical step by identifying many problems that stand in the way of delivering quality systems and services. The management team also identifies solutions to those problems, most of which possess a cultural aspect. The team, in fact, examines the process by which they managed all technical aspects of the department. Improvements to the management process are the foundation upon which technical improvements could be made.

However, has the actual culture of the organization changed by solving management and technical problems, and, if so, how much? What elements in the cultural climate still remain to be addressed?

How can the IS management team know if sufficient action to improve the cultural climate within the department has occurred? What benchmark can be used to evaluate the conditions of the cultural environment? Indeed, if the IS department does embrace the philosophies and principles of TQM, what conditions in the management and cultural arena need to exist for TQM to succeed?

A ready benchmark as a starting point are Deming's famous 14 points. An examination of these points reveals, at least in the experience of Deming, a list of conditions and attitudes needed for improvements in quality and productivity. They provide indicators of an organization dedicated to continuous improvement.

Let us use these 14 points to examine the cultural conditions that exist in the IS department. Let us see how many of these points are applicable, how they can be evidenced, and which of the 14 might prove inappropriate to implement.

By using Deming's 14 points, we are making some assumptions about the nature of computer people in the workplace. Both Deming and TQM, in general, support and advocate Theory Y management. Theory Y advocates, as opposed to Theory X supporters, believe that the vast majority of people want to produce quality work and want to participate in decision making that affects their future. Theory X, on the other hand, purports that most people are lazy, unmotivated, not very creative, and need extremely close supervision. Theory X will most definitely not work with the brand of *knowledge* worker in the IS department.

Deming and the IS Department

Implicit in Deming's famous points is the assumption that employees' goals and objectives are naturally consistent with the goals and objectives of the organization and that the employee will act with understanding and in good faith consistent with objectives which the organization must achieve to meet the customer's requirement.

That is a huge assumption, which in many cases simply is not true."[33]

This chapter began with some thoughts and examples on the difficulty an uncooperative element in a bureaucracy of knowledge workers can cause. These situations result from a misalignment between employee goals and organization goals and objectives. (The author is not so naive as to think that this is always the case, but other mechanisms exist to handle the truly troublesome employee. Aligning the two sets of goals is at the bottom of Deming's 14 points.) Let us apply Deming to the situation and see if improvements can result.

Create Constancy of Purpose for Improvement

No one but the manager can set the goals and aspirations of an organization. Sometimes it is said, "We have to decide what business we are in." This is not enough. The manager must decide what kind of organization the company is to become. The manager must articulate the goals and strategies of the company in such a way that the public, the employees, the vendors, and the customers understand what to expect from the company."[34]

What statement of goals and strategy could be expressed by the IS manager that would demonstrate constancy of purpose? In chapters 2 and 3, questions were posed that would provide such a statement of purpose. It was suggested that any systems activity, current or planned, should be able to show a positive relationship to the following questions:

- What will the activity do to improve the quality of our products and services?

- If the activity is not helping our customer reach quality goals, why are we doing it?

- If the activity is not helping to reduce our cost of quality, why are we doing it?

Though constancy of purpose may seem difficult to maintain while caught in the day-to-day fire fight, such statements, if internalized and expected as a rationale for doing things, provide a long-term strategic direction for all future organizational endeavors. This strategic sense will eventually show the way out of the catch-22 situation that plagues most IS departments today.

Such constancy of purpose sets in motion the eventual reality depicted in Figure 3.2 (on page 41). Such statements, followed by action, prepares the IS department and customers for the implementation of the remaining 13 points within a chosen TQM implementation.

Adopt a New Philosophy

Here we adopt and institutionalize the basic philosophies and principles, as set forth in chapter 2. Simply put, this means adopting a customer focus in all the IS department says and does. As discussed earlier, this focus must be not only on the external customer, but on the internal customer as well! From the external customer we get the requirement and remuneration if the requirement is satisfied. But it is in cooperation with our internal customers that we obtain high efficiencies, greater profit, mutual respect, and job (team) satisfaction. It is through the internal customer that we satisfy the external customer.

This new focus would undoubtedly benefit from some initial public relations work, as we unveil our new quality-conscious, customer-oriented, cost-sensitive IS department. But, more importantly, the words of the new philosophy must be backed up with action, and this can only come by walking the walk of TQM. To do this, we must continue with the 14 points.

Cease to Depend on Inspection

"Only the manager can make the policy decision to place responsibility for quality on the workers and not on an army of inspectors."[35] As we have seen, this means creating a systems development environment where the quality assurance functions of validation, verification, and test are performed at appropriate points throughout the SDP. The SDP, as taught in all its commercial forms, acknowledges the necessity for a phase-by-phase quality assurance activity. The cost of fixing errors and omission (Figure 1.4 on page 8 as well as Figure 2.2 on page 25) shows the results of not enforcing phase-by-phase quality assurance within the SDP. Figure 1.1

(on page 2) shows the results from the customer's point of view. When these IS costs of quality are combined with the costs of quality borne by the customer, the argument for total SDP quality assurance will be much better understood and will be expected by the customer.

Stop Buying on Price Alone

"The practice of purchasing from the lowest bidder as a means to stimulate competition among vendors is destructive to the quest for high quality."[36] Unless quality is factored into the evaluation criteria, low price is too high a price to pay! How to factor quality into the evaluation process is the subject of another book, but a few generalities are worth thinking about.

First, this issue should be of real concern to system integrators who may have little or no control over the quality of source products to be integrated.

Second, the quality of most procured products, unless validated against a stated quality criteria, can only be surmised based on thoroughness of the product's development. In other words, did the developer of the item (that is, hardware, software, or system) actually practice the very things covered in this book? Or, did the developer perform the commonly experienced slipshod work that customers of IS products have come to expect? There is no equivalent to the *Good Housekeeping Seal of Approval* in this business.

Third, the practice of inferring the quality of a product or service based on the academic credentials of those working on the project should be tempered by the realization that management's enforcement or nonenforcement of the SDP discipline far outweighs a room full of degrees. True, the degreed people may know that proper analysis, design, programming, and testing practices are being circumvented, but what are they to do?

Fourth, whether the purchase of hardware, software, or an entire information system supports the quality goals of the IS department or those of the customer is a function of whether requirements are met. Nothing changes with the execution of the SDP phases, except that an additional level of complexity, uncertainty, and risk (that is, the vendors and their products) enters the equation. Far too many automation efforts are carried out as though the purchase of a commercial off-the-shelf something actually made systems delivery easier. And, if the quality and reliability of the purchased item comes into question, a real fiasco is in the making. This has been an all-too-common experience during the last decade.

Improve Process Forever

Improving processes forever is the function of the IS department. Adding value to the business process of the enterprise is the reason for the existence of the department.

How well the IS department meets that demand is dictated by how well the department manages itself and the process whereby it constructs and delivers systems and services to customers. Realization of this point centers around the continuous improvement of the internal management processes.

As we have seen, improvements to these internal management processes create an environment for success in which quality systems constructed for our external customers can be achieved. Improving these management processes requires continual vigilance to ensure that technical issues and fire fighting do not replace

- Planning
- Budgeting
- Organizing
- Staffing
- Directing
- Coordinating
- Controlling
- Reporting

These traditional management functions represent the level of responsibility for IS managers. It is through these functions and processes that management can influence, for good or ill, the quality of information products and services coming from the IS department.

Only when management processes are under review and well on their way to correction should the technical processes used in construction and delivery be tackled. This is because the endless parade of technological widgets needs to be examined with some coherence. Only when the IS department is properly managed and aligned with the quality goals and objectives of the enterprise will such a sense of coherence begin to appear.

This does not mean that the IS department should remain ignorant of new technology; it merely means that new technology should be examined, and certainly utilized, within an envelope of quality goals and managed direction.

Deming's remaining nine points deal exclusively with the human resources of the IS department. The trick is to create a working environment in which these points can become natural to the day-to-day interplay within the organization.

Drive Out Fear

Warren McFarland of Harvard Business School is noted for recommending that any significant change in an enterprise be implemented by a team whose membership includes both sociologists and psychologists. This recommendation is no doubt based on the premise that these professional skills are required to address the human anxiety brought about by change and thereby reduce resistance to that change.

TQM, as a concept, surely suggests change—and to some people change in a big way! If employees or managers believe that by improving quality and increasing productivity their jobs are put in jeopardy, they will resist! They may even do more than resist; they may attempt to sabotage the improvement effort. As was discussed in chapter 1, the average IS professional is very leery today, what with terms like outsourcing, downsizing, rightsizing, and offshore development being bandied about. Is TQM just a cover for one of these?

> Not until the enterprise is demonstrably on the verge of bankruptcy will they accept change. The only way for the management to enlist the worker's help will be to form a genuine partnership in which everyone—workers, supervisors, managers—everyone has the same job security.[37]

Only management can determine the importance it places on each of its five constituencies—self, stockholders, the customer, the public, and the IS employee. The order in which these are regarded and served will be understood from the actions of management, and the IS employee will react and plan accordingly. This is not meant to imply that IS employees expect to see themselves on the top of the list all the time! But it must be clear to them that they are valued and not just considered a meal ticket by top management.

"The degree of trust and confidence required for people to participate in productivity and quality improvements requires more than mere trust. It requires caring and genuine affection."[38] Caring and genuine affection, however, must be demonstrated to be believable. This is a case of *by their works you will know them!* Words must be followed by action!

Institute Leadership

According to Roget's II,[39] to lead is to

- Convince another to adopt a particular belief
- Show the way
- Proceed on a certain course

These are all statements describing the actions of one who leads. It has been said that you manage things; you *lead people*. A military person might say that you lead people into danger—you do not manage them into danger.

The changes brought through the application of TQM philosophies and principles will be viewed, by some, as dangerous. Only leadership can get such individuals past the killer phrases to become willing contributors to quality improvement efforts.

"The managerial orientation, with its emphasis on form over substance, on structure over people and on power relationships over work, is at the heart of the disability of modern business in the United States," writes Abraham Zaleznik, professor emeritus, Harvard Business School.[40] Zaleznik describes a leader as a chief executive "that inspires loyalty with loyalty, unleashes creativity by his/her own creativity and by example drives out the natural tendency in any organization toward complacency and mediocrity."

The presence of these characteristics on a management team would go a long way to drive out the fear of change that employees may perceive in a TQM effort. The challenge is to build a management team that possesses such characteristics.

What behavioral attitudes should be encouraged to bring out leadership abilities in the current management team? More importantly, what abilities should the managers of the future possess so that we can begin to include these abilities in management selection criteria?

Zaleznik cites two intellectual capabilities that he believes essential to the leader. One is the ability to perform *abstract thinking*, to move from concrete experience to a set of generalized ideas and back to concrete experience again in ways that change the way people think about a problem or an opportunity.

The other is *curiosity and openness* to new experiences and ideas, qualities that enable a business leader to empathize with customers, suppliers, or employees and to engage in productive conversations with them on how things can be improved. The leader possesses a vision and shares that vision with everyone.

Finally, a few words of explanation regarding the relationship between the skills of leadership and the emphasis chapter 3 placed on management functions and activities. The point made in chapter 3 was that successful technical quality improvements cannot be made to any business process (that is, the SDP) that is not being competently managed. If the management functions of planning, directing, staffing, and so on are not performed, then an environment for success for technical improvements does not exist and quality/productivity advances will not materialize.

Leadership is required to get the management team to undertake the self-scrutiny necessary to make improvements to the management process. Leadership is required to project the vision and firm belief that TQM endeavors are worth the effort. Leadership is necessary to make TQM real and not just a fad.

A TQM Implementation Model for the IS Department

Of Deming's remaining seven points, the next five are best addressed within a framework that can be used to facilitate their implementation.

- Institute training.
- Break down barriers.
- Eliminate slogans.
- Institute self-improvement.
- Promote continuous improvement.

These five points put people first and are the essence of walking the walk for knowledge workers. Failure to address these five points clearly indicates an unwillingness on the part of management to risk any change of a substantive nature. It means that TQM is just another phase *that management is going through* and that nothing is going to be any different.

At least since the publication of Peters and Waterman's *In Search of Excellence*, discussions of the importance of organizational culture as a means for nurturing enterprise excellence have become commonplace. The culture must provide the psychological support to DRTRFT. But, while such discussions may be commonplace and while TQM provides the necessary philosophies and principles, stories are beginning to unfold about how enterprises, even those that recognize the importance of cultural issues and have embraced TQM, are experiencing difficulty getting past the adrenalin rush of initial program excitement.

This is possibly due to the fact that many TQM activities suggested by the consultant community are not integrating smoothly into the existing management process. In all fairness, few consultants have been asked to participate in such an integration and organizational design effort. The impression that the "nonguru" has is that TQM activities need to either replace present management methods or that somehow TQM must be laminated onto the existing management process.

The answer, of course, is that TQM philosophies and principles cannot replace the existing management process. They are meant to influence current management thinking and change expectations and beliefs about what the organization can do to better satisfy all customers. TQM activities must be integrated into the existing management process. In this way the culture will begin to reflect the philosophies and principles of TQM through the day-to-day management of the organization.

A TQM culture in the IS department should

- Encourage the idea of quality and support the "champions" of the idea

- Foster, and perhaps require, the exchange of innovation and knowledge among personnel and projects on a regular basis

- Encourage and adequately support job/career-related external educational pursuits

- Provide, whenever possible, internal career paths complete with individual training plans to achieve progression through the path

To achieve these goals, internal organizational mechanisms should be initiated to generate and share new ideas, and to formalize for actual use, methods, tools, and techniques, perhaps using the Software Engineering Institute Assessment as a beginning benchmark for tool, technique, and training selection.

The following discussion will provide some ideas concerning mechanisms that could be used by the IS department to assist with TQM implementation and to promote necessary cultural change. In keeping with TQM philosophies, all elements of the IS business process need to be periodically reviewed for continuous improvement.

Figure 7.1 illustrates a continuous process that can be implemented inside an IS department. The process takes the department along the route of doing, checking lessons learned, and, based on those lessons, exploring ways to improve. The major elements of the IS business process that need to be reviewed on a continuous basis include

- The SDP methodology

- Tools and techniques used to construct and deliver systems and services

- Guidelines, instructions, and procedures for the IS department and project management

- Standards, both external and internal, that must be met for final customer acceptance

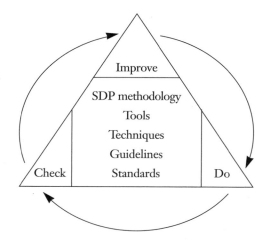

Figure 7.1. Continuous improvement process.

These four elements include systems analysis and design methodologies, namely those that enforce structure as well as automated support tools, such as CASE and automated testing and documentation tools.

Also included in the tools and techniques category are those traditional TQM techniques taken from the manufacturing world that assist in work process analysis, such as

- Benchmarking
- Cause-and-effect diagrams
- Concurrent engineering
- Design of experiments
- Input/output analysis
- Pareto charts
- Statistical analysis
- Workflow analysis

These are well-known techniques covered in all generic TQM implementation training programs. They closely align with and support the techniques already in the IS department tool kit.

The resource for carrying out the continuous review activities is the employees of the IS department, assisted occasionally by outside experts. Figure 7.2 depicts a number of activities and organizational mechanisms for internalizing the five points from Deming that deal with the human elements of the IS department. It is through these activities that the "empowerment" of the employee takes place. Some of these mechanisms come directly from the generic TQM model presented in chapter 2, and some come from the current practices of enlightened IS department structures.

To illustrate the flow and interaction, we begin at the bottom left of the triangle.

Check: Performance of cost-of-quality evaluations on current, completed, or terminated projects will provide the initial raw data on what it costs to get satisfactory products to the customer. These cost-of-quality evaluations will uncover (even without sophisticated metrics) areas within the IS business process that need study and improvement. If the customers are agreeable, the costs of quality they have experienced due

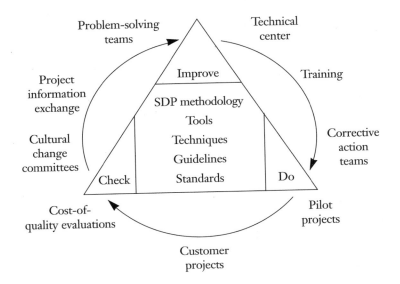

Figure 7.2. Continuous improvement process.

to less-than-desirable information system outputs should also be calculated in order to present a more complete cost picture.

Depending upon the nature of the problems uncovered, three mechanisms are shown for addressing them.

1. If the problem is well understood, the solution clear, and can be easily handled within the existing project management structure, a *project information exchange* approach makes sure that problems and solutions are shared. The project information exchange is a regularly scheduled meeting of project representatives who specialize in particular areas of IS technology. The purpose is to facilitate the discussion of experiences, lessons learned, and techniques across all groups of the IS department. Meeting minutes are recommended so that summary reports can be distributed to all employees. This allows the solution to one problem to benefit other projects where similar problems may arise. Collective reflection at the information exchange sessions also allow preventive actions to be proposed. Agendas for project information exchange meetings should be structured with a systems development or management topic forming the assigned area for discussion. For example, the subject of project documentation would allow each project representative handling documentation activities to present

   - A description of their customer's requirement

   - The SDP and project plans for producing documents that meet the requirement

   - Problems that were/are anticipated with actions taken to prevent or mitigate those problems

   - Lessons learned with suggestions for improving the process of document generation

   - New tools or techniques that should be examined for possible future use

   Project information exchanges provide an excellent forum for improving technical communications between projects and serves to break down barriers between staff areas.

2. TQM *cultural change committees* for solving structural management problems that are preventing an environment for success.

3. TQM problem-solving teams for in-depth examining of SDP work processes, exploring alternative solutions, and proposing corrective actions.

Improve: There are various organizational mechanisms that can be used to carry out the improvement phase of the continuous process. The primary objective of the improvement phase is to evaluate technical recommendations from the previous phase and to implement such recommendations into the IS business process and to conduct training as required. The primary resource for evaluating technical recommendations is IS employees organized into either *corrective action teams* or, in larger IS departments, a *technical center* with a rotating staff. This staff should come from active projects to prevent an ivory tower[41] image from developing and to promote employee involvement with all TQM improvement activities.

Such implementation of problem-solving measures and new technology requires a degree of work process and organizational tailoring; the training conducted in this phase should also be tailored to make it effective. It is usually necessary to use a great deal of prepackaged training, but the objective should be to internalize the training by tailoring it to SDP methodology, tools, techniques, guidelines, and standards as they are actually used within the IS department. Many training dollars are wasted because general purpose training, no matter how professional, is never aligned with the way the IS business process works. Training not presented within the context of the actual work process can lead to many interpretations. If the training in a new tool or technology is not tied to when and how it is to be used, and what effect it has on improving quality, then a major opportunity is missed for cultural change and improving technical effectiveness.

Do: Doing is the continuous improvement aspect where the customer benefits from IS efforts to improve quality. Often *pilot projects*, with full customer knowledge, provide a highly visible and reasonably safe way to introduce change to the SDP, other IS workprocesses, and the customer. Following pilot project completion, an accelerated trip through the cycles of checking and improving can fine-tune the change that was introduced during the pilot. Once fine-tuned, the change is ready for more widespread implementation.

From this description it can be seen that each of the organizational mechanisms of the continuous improvement process provides a number of benefits that are consistent with Deming's five points for employee involvement. This practical process provides a

- Controlled way to address changes in technology
- Way to exchange information at the working level
- Way to standardize practices in systems development
- Way to effect cross training of personnel
- Way to include and gain the support of all willing employees
- Way to rise above slogans to effect lasting change
- Way to institutionalize continuous enhancement to the SDP and other IS workprocesses

These benefits allow the IS department to build a matrix of experts. It provides a way to address technological change in a controlled and timely fashion and provides many possible advancement opportunities for employees.

The remaining two of Deming's 14 points follow:

- Eliminate quotas.
- Remove barriers to self-esteem—eliminate annual ratings.

These are based on his belief that performance quotas, incentive pay systems, and the system of annual merit increases are destructive and counterproductive to morale, performance, teamwork, and quality. Not surprisingly (to anyone who has ever heard him speak) his solution is outright abolition of the offending systems. It is not clear, however, with what the offending systems would be replaced.[42]

Within the typical IS department, the answer, if there is one, is to look to the *rewards and recognition system*. We have seen that work measurement generally causes problems for the IS department, and reward systems work best when work measurement is possible. So until adequate and fair measurement is possible, we have an even more severe problem that can be the use of arbitrary measures and performance quotas coupled to annual ratings!

An initial way to deal with these last two of Deming's points could be to incorporate support for TQM activities into the annual rating criteria. If managers and employees know that support for the program is expected and is being evaluated, the message of seriousness is delivered. If support for TQM is not considered in an evaluation item, another message is sent. We know that people do what is considered important, and what is important is evaluated.

By way of illustration, this same issue of program support has always plagued the computer security arena. Posters, briefings, audits, surveys, and training can only prepare the organization to secure its computer and information assets. But, generally, nothing happens until there is an incident, a security breach, or until top management begins evaluating employees on how well they support and comply with the security program's requirements.

Over time, as the TQM program matures, the evaluation criteria can be refined and aligned with the job functions of the individual employee. This must occur at all levels within the IS department from top executives on down to the trainee.

This concludes the discussion of Deming's 14 points and how they can be used to benchmark the creation of a culture within which total quality principles and philosophies can flourish. Also examined was a continuous improvement process (Figures 7.1 and 7.2) proposing a way in which many of Deming's points can be implemented. The major advantage to implementing such a model is that it begins to institutionalize those points from Deming that put people first.

The mechanisms and activities of the continuous improvement process model are not expensive nor excessively time-consuming when properly administered. They are very effective in demonstrating the seriousness and critical nature of TQM to the organization by

- Demonstrating a long-term commitment on the part of management
- Providing for information exchange and improved communications between projects and individuals

- Integrating the two TQM-unique mechanisms (that is, cultural change committees and problem-solving/corrective action teams) into a broader program of action

- Subjecting the naysayer and reluctant manager and employee to a kind of Chinese water torture approach to implementation—no matter how long it takes, we will *all* participate in a new way of doing business in this organization

- Providing ample opportunity for managers and employees to demonstrate their new behaviors, and for senior executives to show disapproval at negative behavior and reinforce the need and expectation for the new attitudes required for success of the program

Summary and Conclusions

In the first six chapters the focus was on the need for TQM—how it works and its application to the business of IS. As with anything else, successful application of concepts, no matter how compelling the argument, is rooted in the implementation.

For all that TQM can bring to the IS department, it would be unfortunate if the benefits could not be realized for want of an implementation strategy. The continuous improvement process presented in this chapter describes such a strategy and outlines its use. This model incorporates and provides the necessary psychological support for implementing Deming's 14 points.

An honest and energetic attempt to implement this or a similar model will provide the long-term institutional impetus for bringing about the technical quality improvements and the cultural changes required to better serve the customers of the IS department.

8 Possible Futures for an IS Department in a Quality-Conscious Enterprise

Introduction

This final chapter will serve to present two possible futures for an IS department that is expected to deliver systems and services to a quality-conscious enterprise.

The total quality movement has been active for the last six or seven years. Most fads would have come and gone by now. While the initial flush of excitement may have passed, it is being replaced by something far more permanent—the sense that goods and services can be improved and the sense that it must be done and done to last.

In fact, merely to survive, we must do it because of pressures from the global economy. In addition, each of us, as customers with our own evolving quality expectations, is beginning to understand what others are beginning to expect of us as providers of information systems and services.

The *customer–provider–customer* paradigm, coupled with the economic threat from the global marketplace, puts the TQM movement at a level far above the typical management fad. Also, by focusing on cost of quality, TQM provides a different and crucial link to the bottom line, such that necessary investments in quality improvement activities can actually be justified.

Another aspect of TQM that will ensure its survival (although the name may change) is the comprehensiveness of its approach. It is in fact *total* because it causes the examination of all processes by which the enterprise manages and produces its goods and services, while at the same time including the elements of organizational and human resource development that are so often consigned by management to the personnel department. This can be especially true in technology and engineering organizations where few managers have training or experience in personnel management.

Yes, TQM is changing a great many things. Through TQM, our customers are being introduced to a profound (for most organizations) new approach to doing business. This new way of doing business makes it OK to deal with

- Technology
- People
- Relationships
- Feelings
- Power

Through TQM customers are taught to deal continuously with the business and work process problems facing them. They begin to understand that problem solving and continuous improvement, conducted by themselves on the processes of their workplace, will lead to quality and productivity gains that benefit all who are involved.

TQM is changing the degree of employee involvement in how work is to be accomplished. TQM is changing values and TQM is changing the expectations of customers for quality. Customers expect honesty, openness, and cooperation when dealing with each other, their customers, and, hopefully, with their IS providers. These experiences and heightened expectations pose a series of questions that senior IS management must address.

- Because of TQM, what might our customers begin to expect of the IS department?
- How can the IS manager and the department respond?

- How does the IS manager and the organization want to respond?
- How will the IS manager and the department respond?

All futures are potentially possible, we have but to choose![43] So what choice does the IS department and its management team have regarding the questions just posed? There are really only two choices.

1. Seize the opportunities presented by TQM.

2. Experience the consequences of trying to avoid TQM.

At the risk of being negative, but in the interest of motivation, let us explore the consequences of avoidance first and then finish with the array of opportunities afforded the IS department that sees TQM in an advantageous light and aggressively pursues it.

Consequences of Avoiding TQM

In a quality-conscious enterprise where the customer–provider–customer paradigm has taken hold, the customer or provider who does not play by the TQM rules will be seen as part of the problem, not part of the solution. If, in good faith, the rest of the enterprise is attempting to improve quality and productivity, the customer or provider who does not play by the rules of TQM will eventually be considered a hinderance to progress.

In chapter 1 the perceptions of the IS department were not too flattering, but in some ways understandable given the maturity of the industry. If, however, the IS department does not now actively engage their customers in meaningful TQM dialogue concerning quality improvements, the customer will begin to ask, *Who are they, and what do they do?*

This question left unanswered will result in a loss of support from customers and other sponsors. This means that if the value added by the IS department is not clearly perceived by the customer, the IS department, in a government agency, becomes harder and harder to defend at budget time. Or, in a commercial fee for service environment, customers begin to exercise their options to shop around for better, higher quality information systems and services.

In either case the IS manager and organization begin to lose control over their organization and their future. One of the major challenges of most IS departments in the next decade will be to get off overhead and be seen as a key contributor to the value-added side of the ledger. TQM can make this possible!

Unprecedented Opportunities
On the other hand, by energetically embracing TQM, a message can be sent to all of our customers that the IS department acknowledges its own difficulties with quality and addresses them in the same disciplined fashion that has become familiar throughout the rest of the enterprise. From this initial action the following opportunities present themselves and great benefits begin to accrue for the IS department and the enterprise.

Create Partnerships of Mutual Benefit
By embracing TQM the IS department plays to its analytic strengths and can become a truly indispensable factor in a program that has a profound effect on the customers as they begin to redesign their business work processes. In earlier chapters the linchpin phenomenon was explored, and it was seen that the tools and techniques commonly provided to our customers through TQM are largely systems analysis and design tools that have long been in the tool kit of the systems developer. Further, it was seen that other organizational elements of the enterprise can only progress to a certain point in their TQM workprocess analysis before they run up against automation.

Since TQM and information systems development both focus on process, an unprecedented opportunity exists to reach out to the customer with assistance during the customer's quality improvement efforts.

As discussed earlier, the complementary relationship depicted in Figure 5.1 (on page 62) is what the IS department and customer should strive for as business redesign begins. As the figure shows, each of the three analysis activities complement each other and provide a more comprehensive understanding of the business area being examined within the context of the enterprise. Vaughan Merlyn says, "If aligning information systems with business goals is the objective, TQM is the ideal methodology to achieve it."[44]

From the IS perspective a number of advantages can be realized. First, the customer, having been introduced to the process focus of TQM, is much better equipped to participate when automated process questions are posed during any future analysis effort. For the IS analyst, this may be the first time that customers have been even remotely prepared to deal with the level of detail needed to defined an automated requirement. This is because the customer has been sensitized and taught to think in process terms. The customer is similarly prepared to answer questions concerning quality attributes and to define final systems acceptance criteria.

Second, by using the model and language of TQM, a neutral frame of reference is available to the IS analyst in explaining the many demands of information systems analysis and design. For example, the SDP itself and its many seemingly unnecessary steps can be explained in the TQM language of

- Meeting requirements
- Error-free work
- Managing by prevention
- Measurement/cost of quality
- Problem-solving/corrective action

Remembering that the SDP is a TQM-compatible process for defining and constructing a quality information system, the necessary steps of the SDP can be explained more effectively to any customer in the language of TQM rather than in the IS lingo of IE, RAD, JAD, CASE, and so on.

This means, of course, that the IS analyst must be conversant with TQM principles and language so that the necessary translations can be made. In many instances IS department involvement will include the actual decipherment of what current automated systems are doing, as well as the use of graphic software tools (for example, CASE) to capture and document the customer's TQM deliberation—the real beginning of business process redesign. In practice our opportunity to reach out will occur naturally once the IS department makes clear its offer to actively participate in the TQM initiatives of the customer.

A word of caution! We cannot keep changing the language of management every year or so. We cannot keep changing the language of systems analysis and design every year or so. We merely offer ready-made excuses for some individuals to wait and do nothing. We have all the concepts, principles, tools, and techniques that we need. We need to pull all the methodologies together and focus on the customer.

Change Perceptions Through Performance

The IS department's sphere of influence is great and the potential to assist customers in their quest for quality is major. However, aggressively embracing TQM and becoming active with customers in their pursuit of workprocess improvement can only go so far in changing the perceptions the customer has of the IS department.

As seen earlier, Figure 3.2 (on page 41) depicts a reality where, until the IS department turns inward and appreciably improves its own workprocesses, the systems and services affecting customers will not improve. Without such direct improvement being shown, customer perceptions will not change.

In other words, the improvement in customer relations brought about through the reach-out activities described above must be quickly supported by improved quality of IS products across the board. This means getting the internal IS house in order.

Identification of IS internal workprocesses needing improvement will, of course, come about through the TQM techniques of cost-of-quality analysis, measurement activities, and the initial management process analysis done by the management team. But another, more visible, way to jump-start the effort would be to capitalize on the new relationship being forged with customers. Through surveys and meetings solicit their ideas on how the IS department can improve service.

This can be as simple as asking three questions of the IS customer.

- What part of the work output and support service helps you meet your job requirements the first time every time?

- What elements of the work output or support service inhibit your ability to meet your job requirements the first time?

- What additional needs do you have that we might be able to provide that would help you meet your job requirement?

Offering to assist customers with their TQM workprocess deliberations and asking them how we can improve our day-to-day service, will, to paraphrase Mark Twain, gratify some people and astonish the rest. These two actions will result in a significant change in the attitude of most customers toward the IS department and will create a situation in which additional improvement opportunities begin to present themselves.

Add Value to the Enterprise

Once the relationship between the IS provider and the customer has begun redefinition, the opportunities for value-added consultations increase dramatically.

Premise: Given their choice, the enterprise's internal customers would prefer to deal with the IS department rather than with outside contractors. This is especially the case if it appears that the department has a real concern for quality and a genuine interest in the customer.

Many IS customers are tired of the care and feeding game and would be happy to just do their job and stop doing the technician's job as well. As the IS customer/provider relationship improves, the IS department can begin to

- Provide *trusted* consultations to customers regarding technology. Trusted refers to the sense that technology consultations can be viewed as less self-serving if coming from within the enterprise than from outside.

- Sensitize the customer regarding the great complexities and uncertainties that accompany most automation initiatives. Such discussions, conducted in the language of TQM, will stand in stark contrast to the smooth, no-problem approach of many vendors and contractors. It will be seen by the customer as more truthful when it originates from a team player who has the customer's quality interests at heart.

- Perform assessments on future technologies that may affect the customer's workprocess and products. This activity can add great value to the enterprise if it results in a competitive advantage.

- Conduct assessments that uncover immature and insupportable technologies that could pose future problems and risks for the customer.

Through all of these activities, the IS department and its customers are working in partnership to improve the quality of enterprise goods and services with the use of automation consigned to its important but properly supporting role. This then leads to two additional opportunities for the IS department.

Formulate a Long-Term TQM Vision

Based on commonly derived quality goals, the IS department and its customers can begin to formulate a joint vision of where technology can take the enterprise.

Associated with this vision, a technical strategy can be articulated that supports the business goals of the customer. Historically, this vision has been called the information systems plan, and it has attempted to relate technological support initiatives to the business plan of the enterprise. Most often, the information systems plan relates to nothing the customer is really doing and merely reflects the wishes of the IS department.

The new quality partnership between the IS department and its customers should improve the value of future planning documents since the picture presented will be much more comprehensive. These plans will have the following characteristics.

- Reflect the results of having conducted concurrent information requirements analysis and business area TQM workprocess deliberations.

- Represent the total system requirements depicted by Figure 1.3 (on page 6).

- Present a sociotechnical picture of the business area system.

- Present a much more comprehensive economic analysis since the cost-of-quality studies will argue for improvements that in the past were not justifiable or could be dismissed as intangible. The cost of quality adds a new and powerful dimension to the whole issue of cost/benefit justifications and should be used to advantage.

- Present a more coherent picture of technological support to the business processes of the enterprise.

As this key contribution the IS department can make to the enterprise begins to emerge, sponsorship and support for the IS department will improve.

Obtain Customer Support for IS Department Infrastructure Investments

Based on the joint TQM vision and working relationship between the IS department and the customer, the IS executive can better justify current and desired technological investments, initiatives, practices, and other needed changes. Quality improvements being made to the customer's workprocess through joint analysis will serve as justification for customer improvements (for example, redesigned business systems) and IS department infrastructure improvements as well (for example, new methods, tools, software, training, etc.). The need to garner customer support for continuous improvements to the infrastructure will be much easier if the customer, for example, can attest to a relationship between a new CASE tool and the improved quality of an information system or service that supports meeting the customer's business goals.

In a fee for service environment such infrastructure improvements can be difficult to justify without an understanding on the part of customers. Infrastructure enhancements that improve the quality of systems may add expense and, therefore, must be offset by the knowledge that value will be added to customer's workprocess with business area quality or productivity increases resulting.

The quantification of benefits resulting from IS infrastructure enhancements is best accomplished in cooperation with the users of our work products: the customer.

Management of the IS Department Is Simplified

While this may seem to be an implausible statement, such is not the case. TQM simplifies the management of the IS department because it concentrates management focus on the customer and the cost of quality. With this focus it is possible to view all current activities and planned initiatives through this simple yet effective lens.

- If the activity or initiative is not contributing to quality information systems and services, why are we doing it?

- If the activity or initiative is not helping our customers reach their quality goals, why are we doing it?

It is also possible to view these same activities and initiatives through the cost of quality lens.

- If the activity or initiative is not improving our cost of quality profile (that is, reducing rework, scrap, and so on), why are we doing it? By inference this would also include cost of quality improvements hoped for by the customer.

No one ever set out to build a poor quality system. It happens because management's focus has been diverted away from effectively and efficiently meeting customer requirements.

A higher-quality, cost-effective direction can be reestablished for the IS department if senior management makes its decisions with paramount sensitivity to the three questions posed above.

Steps for Getting Started or How to Resuscitate Your TQM Efforts

This final discussion will center on some initial actions that need to be taken to ensure the success of a TQM effort. It is based on the following concepts that have formed the foundations for this book.

- TQM is not a fad but a management method that will become more prominent during the remainder of this decade.

- TQM seeks to improve the way we work by examining the processes whereby work is accomplished.

- A work process that TQM examines is highly likely to be dependent on automation.

- Significant improvement to work processes that are dependent on automation will be unlikely without the full involvement of the IS department.

- There is a direct relationship between the quality of systems and services and the quality of goods and services that the enterprise produces.

- There is a similar direct relationship between cost of producing systems and services and the cost that IS customers experience in producing their own goods and services. Major reductions in these combined costs can result by improving the quality of IS work processes.

- The SDP is TQM-compatible and typifies the principal work-process of the IS department. As such, it must be the prime target of the continuous improvement program under TQM.

- Many opportunities exist for the IS department that embraces TQM, uses it to improve the quality of its systems and services, and capitalizes on it as the medium for forging new quality-oriented relationships with their customers.

Announce Intention to Begin a TQM Effort

First, the IS executive must announce his or her intention to begin a TQM program. This announcement must convey a sense of conviction that the program is essential and needed to improve systems and service products that customers depend on to meet their quality objectives.

This effort should begin with an intervention by professional TQM facilitators. This process should definitely be used to help the IS management team identify and resolve its structural management problems and to create the environment for success. This approach will also ensure a properly balanced sociotechnical design to the institutional mechanisms needed to manage a successful implementation within the IS department. This intervention would probably be more effective if the TQM facilitators have familiarity and management experience in the IS business.

For IS departments that have already initiated TQM programs, it may be a good time to examine the extent of implementation to see if tangible progress is being made. If the effort appears to have stalled, it is either because management commitment is being tested or because insufficient thought has been given to implementing mechanisms. It may also be that insufficient attention has been given to existing structural management problems. If so, these problems are undoubtedly preventing program progress and quality improvements. Regardless of program condition or progress, revitalization can occur as easily and in as short a time as it takes the IS executive to renew walking the walk.

Walking the walk at the executive level means fighting to stay above the day-to-day crisis, and forcing the organization to focus on its purpose and work products.

Create an Active TQM Posture: Reach Out!

The real benefit to both the IS department and the customer of systems and services comes through partnership. The nature of the service (that is, information and systems in support of business activity) requires the closest possible collaboration.

The IS department needs the trust, support, goodwill, and understanding of the customer. The customer, on the other hand, needs reliable information and systems at a reasonable cost, and the peace of mind that results from dependable customer service.

It may be that the perception of the IS department is generally low in the mind of the customer—all the more reason to seize the opportunities offered by TQM to improve that perception. Remember, *all futures are possible; we have but to chose!*

Remembering also the customer/provider relationship, the first steps probably should be taken by the IS executive toward the customer. It is incumbent upon the IS executive to define and establish this relationship. It is desirable that this be done before customers pressure the IS department to get on board the TQM train. It is imperative that this be done before customers consider abandoning the IS department in favor of other IS providers.

Work on Image—Consider a PR Effort

A major aspect of this new relationship must be to inform customer management of how current IS department practices and planned initiatives actually support everyone's desire for quality improvement. As part of a public relations effort, a series of presentations should be developed that clearly show why the SDP is TQM-compatible and how it is in the best interest of both the customer and the IS department to jointly support its use and adherence on all projects. Here, the ability to explain the SDP in the language of TQM will ensure a more favorable reception and understanding than if explained in IS jargon.

A primary objective for such a presentation would be to show that while the IS department acknowledges problems with quality, it does not concede that poor quality systems and service are its sole responsibility. The two-way duty for customer/provider communications must be made clear and be shown as critical to the likelihood of success for final system or service delivery. This concept, stated in TQM language, will be understood—perhaps for the first time.

Map Current IS Department Practices
Against TQM Principles

A possible aid in setting direction for the new, quality-conscious IS department would be to inventory current practices, procedures, and new initiatives, and map them against the major principles of TQM. It will have an encouraging effect on employees, as well as on the customer, to learn that the tools, techniques, and methodologies they are now using support quality system construction. Included in this analysis would be a section showing how desired and needed methods (for example, information engineering), tools (for example, CASE), and techniques (for example, validation, verification, and testing), could support and make possible the delivery of improved quality information systems and services. This analysis should also make it clear that TQM will not cause any major upheavals, but that successful quality improvement can result from a new focus, a new way of thinking, and persistence.

Summary and Conclusions

In this final chapter two possible futures for an IS organization have been presented—one negative, the other positive. To the extent that customer perceptions of the IS department are low (chapter 1) and the

IS department does not move aggressively to embrace the philosophies and principles of TQM, the future outlook will be bleak. This future will prove the saying, *If you do what you always did, you'll get what you always got!*

If, on the other hand, an IS department recognizes the need for quality improvement, embraces the philosophies and principles of TQM, and exerts the necessary effort, the future can be extremely bright. This is a future in which the IS department can take its rightful position alongside other organizational elements and be viewed as indispensable to the future success of the enterprise. This, all because of a desire to prove that nobody does it better.

References

1. Daniel Borgen and Michael Silverman, "Manager's Journal," *ComputerWorld* (February 19, 1991): 45.

2. Julia King, "Executive Report: No Safety in Numbers," *ComputerWorld* (March 30, 1992): 85, 86.

3. Ibid.

4. Peter Drucker, *Managing for the Future* (New York: Truman Talley Books, 1992): 96, 97.

5. Ibid.

6. From *Managing for the Future* by Peter Drucker. © 1992 by Peter Drucker. A Truman Talley Book. Used by permission of Dutton Signet, a division of Penguin Books USA Inc. 100, 101, 102.

7. John Van, "Customers Want to See It in Dollars," *Chicago Tribune* (November 17, 1991): sec. 19, p. 1.

8. See note 2 above.

9. Irv Wendell, "Executive Report: Opinion Poll," *ComputerWorld* (March 30, 1992): 85.

10. Copyright 1992. Reprinted with permission from *ComputerWorld.*

11. *Webster's New World Dictionary,* Third College Edition (Springfield, MA: Merriam-Webster, 1988).

12. President's Council on Management Improvement (PCMI), *Managing the Risk and Uncertainty of Technological Change* (Washington, D.C., 1990): 3.

13. Ken Eason, *Information Technology and Organizational Change* (London: Taylor and Francis, 1988): 12, 33, 35.

14. Richard Baskerville, *Designing Information Systems Security* (Chichester, U.K.: John Wiley & Sons, 1988).

15. Dennis Noonan, "Information Technology: Promises Remain Unfulfilled," *ComputerWorld* (February 18, 1991): 25.

16. Ibid.

17. Robert N. Charette, *Applications Strategies for Risk Analysis* (New York: McGraw-Hill, 1990).

18. Barry Boehm, *Software Engineering Economics* (Englewood Cliffs, N.J.: Prentice Hall, 1981).

19. Software Engineering Institute, *Characterizing the Software Process: A Maturity Framework* (Pittsburgh: Carnegie-Mellon University, 1987): 2.

20. Ibid.

21. Les Ott, "A Mechanism to Achieve the SEI Goals." Paper presented at IDEF Users Conference (May 1992): 10.

22. Robert N. Charette, *Applications Strategies for Risk Analysis,* 1990, McGraw-Hill, Inc. Reproduced with permission of McGraw-Hill, pages 169–180.

23. ANSI/IEEE Std 729-1983 (New York: Institute of Electrical and Electronics Engineers, 1983).

24. Vern Crandall, Ph.D., *How to Reduce the Software Development of Life Cycle* (Provo, Utah: Brigham Young University, 1991): 21.

25. Boris Beizer, *The Frozen Keyboard: Living with Bad Software* (Blue Ridge Summit, Pa.: TAB Books, 1988): 31, 33, 36.

26. Reprinted by written permission of the author from Boris Beizer, *The Frozen Keyboard: Living with Bad Software*, TAB Books, Inc., Blue Ridge Summit, Pa. 1988. pages 33–34.

27. Reprinted by written permission of the author from Boris Beizer, *The Frozen Keyboard: Living with Bad Software*, TAB Books, Inc., Blue Ridge Summit, Pa. 1988. pages 37–38.

28. Jim Hagedon and Chris Durney, *The Context for Case: Building a Productive Development Environment* (Rockville, Md.: Chartway Technologies, 1988): 6.

29. See note 13 above.

30. *American Programmer*, published by Cutter Information Corp., 37 Broadway, Arlington, MA. 02174, USA; 617-641-5118; Fax 617-648-1950. page 26.

31. Ibid.

32. M. Cherlin, *The Toll of Turnover* (Newton, Mass.: DataMotion, 1981): 209.

33. J. Michael Crouch, *An Ounce of Application Is Worth a Ton of Abstraction* (Greensboro, N.C.: LEADS Corporation, 1992): 245.

34. Myron Tribus, *Deming's Redefinition of Management* (Cambridge, Mass.: MIT, 1989): 1, 7, 9, 10.

35. Ibid.

36. Ibid.

37. Ibid.

38. Ibid.

39. *Roget's II New Thesaurus*, American Heritage Dictionary (Boston: Houghton Mifflin Company, 1980).

40. Abraham Zaleznick, *The Managerial Mystique* (New York: Harper Collins, 1988).

41. "A place of mental withdrawal from reality and action." *Roget's II New Thesaurus, American Heritage Dictionary* (Boston: Houghton Mifflin, 1980).

42. See note 32.

43. Unknown.

44. Vaughan Merlyn, "Final Word," *Information Week* (October 26, 1992): 40.

Bibliography

Baskerville, Richard. *Designing Information Systems Security.* Chichester, U.K.: John Wiley & Sons, 1988.

Beizer, Boris. *The Frozen Keyboard: Living with Bad Software.* Blue Ridge Summit, Pa.: TAB Books, 1988.

Birrel, N. D., and M. A. Ould. *A Practical Handbook for Software Development.* Cambridge, U.K.: Cambridge University Press, 1985.

Boehm, Barry W. *Software Engineering Economics.* Englewood Cliffs, NJ: Prentice-Hall, 1981.

Carzo, Rocco, and Yanouzas, John. *Formal Organization, A Systems Approach.* Homewood, Ill.: Irwin-Dorsey, 1967.

Charette, Robert N. *Applications Strategies for Risk Analysis.* New York: McGraw-Hill, 1990.

Cotterman, William, and James Senn. *Challenges and Strategies for Research in Systems Development.* Chichester, U.K.: John Wiley & Sons, 1992.

Covey, Stephen R. *The 7 Habits of Highly Effective People.* New York: Simon & Schuster, 1989.

Crouch, J. Michael. *An Ounce of Application Is Worth a Ton of Abstraction.* Greensboro, N.C.: LEADS Corporation, 1993.

DeMarco, Tom, and Timothy Lister. *Peopleware: Productive Projects and Teams.* New York: Dorset House, 1987.

Dobyns, Lloyd, and Clare Crawford-Mason. *Quality or Else—The Revolution in World Business.* Boston: Houghton Mifflin, 1991.

Eason, Ken. *Information Technology and Organizational Change,* London: Taylor & Francis, 1988.

Heider, John. *The Tao of Leadership.* New York: Bantam Books, 1985.

Jones, Meilir Page. *Practical Project Management: Restoring Quality to Projects and Systems.* New York: Dorset House, 1985.

Mandell, Steven. *Computer, Data Processing and the Law.* St. Paul, Minn.: West Publishing Company, 1984.

Martin, James. *Strategic Data Planning Methodologies.* Englewood Cliffs, N.J.: Prentice Hall, Inc., 1982.

Martin, James, and Carma McClure. *Structured Techniques for Computing.* Englewood Cliffs, N.J.: Prentice-Hall, 1985.

Naisbitt, John, and Patricia Aburdene. *Re-Inventing the Corporation.* New York: Warner Books, 1985.

Ould, Martyn A. *Strategies for Software Engineering: The Management of Risk and Quality.* New York: John Wiley & Sons, 1990.

Optner, Stanford L. *Systems Analsyis for Business Management.* Englewood Cliffs, N.J.: Prentice-Hall, 1968.

Perry, William. *A Standard for Testing Application Software.* Boston: Auerbach Publishers, 1990.

Peters, Thomas, and Robert Waterman. *In Search of Excellence.* New York: Harper & Row, 1982.

Sherer, Susan A. *Software Failure Risk: Measurement and Management.* New York: Plenum Press, 1992.

Schindler, Max. *Computer-Aided Software Design.* New York: John Wiley & Sons, 1990.

Townsend, Robert. *Further Up the Organization.* New York: Harper and Row, 1984.

Tucker, Robert B. *Managing the Future.* New York: Berkley Books, 1991.

Walton, Mary. *The Deming Management Method.* New York: Perigee Books, 1992.

Whitten, Jeffrey L., Lonnie D. Bentley, and Victor M. Barlow. *Systems Analysis and Design Methods.* Homewood, Ill.: Irwin, 1989.

Index

141